FORERUNNERS: IDEAS FIRST FROM THE UNIVERSITY OF
MINNESOTA PRESS

Original e-works to spark new scholarship

FORERUNNERS IS A thought-in-proces~
works. Written between fresh idea
draws on scholarly work initiated
conference plenaries, journal articl
exchange. This is gray literature pub ___ng,
change, and speculation take place i.

Dark Deleuze

Dark Deleuze

Andrew Culp

University of Minnesota Press

MINNEAPOLIS

Published by the University of Minnesota Press, 2016
111 Third Avenue South, Suite 290
Minneapolis, MN 55401-2520
http://www.upress.umn.edu

The University of Minnesota is an equal-opportunity educator and employer.

Contents

Abbreviations

WORKS BY GILLES DELEUZE

P	*Proust and Signs* (2000)
PI	*Pure Immanence* (2005)
S	*Expressionism in Philosophy: Spinoza* (1990)
TR	*Two Regimes of Madness* (2007)

WORKS BY GILLES DELEUZE AND
FÉLIX GUATTARI

AO	*Anti-Oedipus* (1977)
K	*Kafka: Toward a Minor Literature* (1986)
TP	*A Thousand Plateaus* (1987)
WP	*What Is Philosophy?* (1994)

Introduction

SUMMARIZING HIS DEEPLY IDIOSYNCRATIC WORK, French philosopher Gilles Deleuze describes writing about others as "a sort of buggery" or "immaculate conception" that is the result of "taking an author from behind and giving him a child" (N, 6). Deleuze is still quick to distinguish his project from outright falsification. He strictly limits himself to what an author actually says; he attends to a thinker's "shifting, slipping, dislocations, and hidden emissions" to give him "a child that would be his own offspring, yet monstrous" (N, 6). More than thirty years after making these remarks, Deleuze now has plenty of little monsters of his own—rootless rhi-zombies, dizzying metaphysicians, skittish geonaturalists, enchanted transcendentalists, passionate affectivists. My aim is to give him another child that shares his last name: "Dark Deleuze."

Deleuze once told a friend that a "worthwhile book" performs at least three functions: polemics, recovery, and creativity. In writing the book, the author must reveal that (1) other scholarship commits an error; (2) an essential insight has been missed; and (3) a new concept can be created. You will find all three is this book. First, I argue against the "canon of joy" that celebrates Deleuze as a naively affirmative thinker of connectivity. Second, I rehabilitate the destructive force of negativity

I

by cultivating a "hatred for this world." Third, I propose a conspiracy of contrary terms that diverge from the joyous task of creation.

Picking out a particular strain of thought: scholars of "new materialism" turn to realist ontology by way of Deleuze's metaphysics of positivity. The basis for the realist side of Deleuze is perhaps best evinced by his biography. Those who knew Deleuze consistently note his firm commitment to joyful affirmation and his distaste for the *ressentiment* of negativity. Beatifying this sentiment, Deleuze has been used to establishing a whole canon of joy. In the canon of joy, the cosmos is a complex collection of assemblages produced through the ongoing processes of differentiation. The effect of the Joyous Deleuze's image of thought is a sense of wonder, accompanied by the enjoyment of creating concepts that express how the world really exists.

A different Deleuze, a darker one, has slowly cast its shadow. Yet this figure only appears when we escape the chapel choir of joy for the dark seclusion of the crypt. Emerging from scholars concerned with the condition of the present, the darkness refashions a revolutionary Deleuze: revolutionary negativity in a world characterized by compulsory happiness, decentralized control, and overexposure. This refashioned Deleuze forms a countercanon out of the perfused negativity of his concepts and affects. On the level of concept, it recognizes that negativity impregnates Deleuze's many prefixes of difference, becoming, movement, and transformation, such as *de-*, *a-*, *in-*, and *non-*. On the level of affect, it draws on Deleuze's talk of indiscernibility, concealment, the shame of being human, and the monstrous power of the scream. The ultimate task of this approach is not the creation of concepts, and to the extent that it does, Dark Deleuze creates concepts only to write apocalyptic science fiction (DR, xx–xxii).

Timely Connections

Michel Foucault half-jokingly suggested in 1970 that "perhaps one day, this century will be known as Deleuzian" ("Theatrum Philosophicum," 885). It is easy to see how boosters have used this phrase to raise the profile of Deleuze, who was far less popular than Foucault or Derrida during the initial reception of poststructuralism in America. But what if it is a subtle jab? Foucault makes the remark in the same breath as a reference to Pierre Klossowski, a crucial member of the secret society Acéphale, which helped revive Nietzsche in France when others too easily dismissed the thinker as fascist. "Historically fitting" would be an insult to Nietzsche, who proudly proclaims the untimeliness of thought "acting counter to our time and thereby acting on our time and, let us hope, for the benefit of a time to come" at the beginning of his essay on the uses and abuses of history for life (*Untimely Meditations*, 60). As a major French interlocutor of Nietzsche, Deleuze uses this exact same phrase on untimeliness in the opening pages of *Difference and Repetition*—the very book that Foucault was reviewing when he made the comment. Bearing out the implication by mincing another Nietzschean phrase, then perhaps Foucault was accusing him of being "timely, all too timely."

What would make Deleuze's thought especially timely? Critics such as Slavoj Žižek accuse him of being a poster child for the cultural excesses of postmodern capitalism ("Ongoing 'Soft Revolution'"). A recent round of denunciations underwritten by a mix of wonderment and red-baiting exclaim, "The founder of BuzzFeed wrote his senior thesis on the Marxism of Deleuze and Guattari!," adding to a long list of guilty associations—"the Israeli Defense Force reads *A Thousand Plateaus*!," "Deleuze spouts the fashionable nonsense of pseudoscience!" Deleuze's defenders are correct to dismiss such criticisms as either incomplete or outright spurious. Yet there is a kernel of truth that goes back to an old joke—a communist is someone who reads *Das Kapital*; a capitalist is someone who reads *Das Kapital* and understands it. Saying the same about Deleuze: there is something absolutely essential about his work, but it would not be best to take it at face value. The necessity of "taking another step" beyond Deleuze avant la lettre is especially true when both capitalists and their opponents simultaneously cite him as a major influence. The exact rapport between Deleuze's thought and our time thus remains a puzzle for us to solve. Does the problem arise because certain readers act like doctors who participate in death penalty executions, who follow protocol to make a perfectly clinical diagnosis, only to help administer a set of drugs condemned by their field? Or is there something about his prescription that only exacerbates our current condition?

Ours is the age of angels, says French philosopher Michel Serres (*Angels, a Modern Myth*). Armies of invisible messengers now crisscross the skies, tasked with communication, connection, transmission, and translation. As inspiring as they may seem, they also compel us to embody their messages in word and act. Click, poke, like. We feel the nervous prick of incoming missives that set us in a feverish state until we address the incoming text message, reply to the overdue e-mail, or respond to the pending friend request. These everyday behaviors show that the seemingly modern world of commodities has not stolen our sense of wonder—we are as divinely moved by media as we once were by angels. Marx, who, in Artaud's phrase, has "done away with the judgment of God," shows that this mystical character of the commodity is capitalism and also its most popular trick. Let us then follow Marx's old mole in the search of history, moving from the heavens to the underground. Refusing to sing the hymns of the age, Deleuze and Guattari made a crucial declaration in 1991 as the Iron Curtain crumbled and the first commercial Internet service providers came online: "We do not lack communication. On the contrary, we have too much of it. . . . *We lack resistance to the present*" (WP, 108).

Dark Deleuze's immediate target is connectivity, the name given to the growing integration of people and things through digital technology. Acolyte of connection and Google chairman Eric Schmidt recently declared at the World Economic Forum that soon "the internet will disappear" as it becomes inseparable from our very being ("it will be part of your presence all the time") *(Business Insider)*. This should raise suspicion. No one should ever take futurologists at their word—technology progresses with the same combined and uneven gait as all other types development. Yet the numbers behind Schmidt's claim are hardly a matter of dispute. Five billion new people are slated to join the Internet in the next decade, and the "Internet of things" has motivated individual users to integrate a vast array of online-enabled devices into their everyday lives. Even if they do not fully realize his dreams, they still make up the substance of Google's government of things and the living.

Many traditional concerns have been raised about connectivity. Almost all use the conservative voice of moral caution. A band of "Net Critics" warn that technology is developing more quickly than our understanding of its effects. Popular media, the great screen of the collective unconscious, materialize fears about runaway technology. There is a whole string of Asian horror films that depict cursed media objects ruining our lives *(Ringu, Pulse, Phone, One Missed Call, White: The Melody of the Curse)*. The usual cottage industry of romanticizing life without technology now suggests that "cell phones make us lazy," while circulating ideas on how to "get on a social media diet." Some philosophers, such as Bernard Stiegler, even say that technology is stealing our precious insides. Behind these suggestions lurks a drive to get back to our roots.

The "mad scientist" criticism of technology misses the mark. The trouble is not that myopic technicians have relentlessly pursued technical breakthroughs without considering the consequences ("forgive them, for they know not what they do"; Žižek, *The Sublime Object of Ideology,* 28). The antidote for such ignorance would just be a small dose of ideology critique. Alternatively, technology has not exceeded humanity's capacity to manage it—if anything, Foucault's insights (the analytic of finitude, biopower) suggest that humanity influences its own future more than ever before (DI, 90–93). The problem is, *they know perfectly well what they are doing, but they continue doing it anyway*!

Philosophically, connectivity is about world-building. The goal of connectivity is to make everyone and everything part of a single world. The cases made for such a world are virtuous enough—Kantian cosmopolitanism wants perpetual peace, Marxist universalism demands the unity of theory and practice, and Habermas would have us all be part of one great conversation. Yet connectivity today is determined far more by people like Google Ideas director Jared Cohen, who demonstrates the significance of Deleuze's argument that "technology is social before it is technical" (F, 17). Trained as a counterterrorism expert, Google poached Cohen from a position at the Department of State, where he convinced Condoleezza Rice to integrate social media into the Bush administration's "diplomatic tool kit" (Rice, *No Higher Honor,* 305). In a geopolitical manifesto cowritten with then Google CEO Eric Schmidt, *The New Digital Age,* Cohen reveals Google's deep aspiration to extend U.S. government interests at home and abroad. Their central tool? Connectivity.

When connectivity is taken as a mantra, you can see its effects everywhere. Jobseekers are told to hop on to the web ("While your resume can help you get the interview for a new job, a fully optimized LinkedIn profile can bring you more business, more connections, and can increase your professional reputation!"). Flat hierarchies are touted as good for business management ("Power is vertical; potential is horizontal!"). And the deluge of digital content is treated as the world's greatest resource, held back only by unequal access ("Information wants to be free!"). As perverse as it sounds, many Deleuzians still promote concepts that equally motivate these slogans: transversal lines, rhizomatic connections, compositionist networks, complex assemblages, affective experiences, and enchanted objects. No wonder Deleuze has been derided as the lava lamp saint of "California Buddhism"—so many have reduced his rigorous philosophy to the mutual appreciation of difference, openness to encounters in an entangled world, or increased capacity through synergy.

Instead of drawing out the romance, *Dark Deleuze* demands that we kill our idols. The first task is negative, as in Deleuze and Guattari's schizoanalysis, a "complete currettage"—*overthrow their altars, and break their pillars, and burn their groves with fire; and ye shall hew down the graven images of their gods, and destroy the names of them out of that place* (AO, 311). Put more modestly, the first step is to acknowledge that the unbridled optimism for connection has failed. Temporary autonomous zones have become special economic zones. The material consequences of connectivism are clear: the terror of exposure, the diffusion of power, and the oversaturation of information. A tempting next move would be to criticize Deleuzian connectivists as falling behind the times, having not recognized their own moment of recuperation. Yet such an accusation would only prepare the ground for a more timely intervention. *Dark Deleuze* does not take up the mantle of prophetic guruism or punctual agitprop. As a project, it instead follows Deleuze's ad-

7

vice to create untimely "vacuoles of non-communication" that break circuits rather than extend them (D, 175). The point is not to get out of this place but to cannibalize it—we may be *of* this world, but we are certainly not *for* it. Such out-of-jointedness is a distance. And distance is what begins the dark plunge into the many worlds eclipsed by the old.

Hatred for This World

"We need reasons to believe in this world," Deleuze demands (C2, 172). We are so distracted by the cynicism of ideological critique that we too easily dismiss the real world as an illusion. The problem is exaggerated even more now that we mistake knowledge for belief, a confusion fed by growing databases of readily available information. He asks us to relink with the world as a matter of faith, to believe in something even as transient as the fleeting sensations of cinema (C2, 169–173). Although his suggestion is not wrong, it is incomplete. In his haste, Deleuze forgets to pose the problem with the ambivalence found in all his other accounts of power—how affects are ruled by tyrants, molecular revolutions made fascist, and nomad war machines enrolled to fight for the state. Without it, he becomes Nietzsche's braying ass, which says yes only because it is incapable of saying no (NP, 178–86). We must then make up for Deleuze's error and seek the dark underside of belief. The key to identifying what lies beneath begins with the path of belief, but only to pursue a different orientation. So start with a similar becoming-active that links up with the forces that autoproduce the real. But instead of simply appreciating the forces that produce the World, *Dark Deleuze* intervenes in them to destroy it. At one time, such an intervention would have been called the Death of God, or more recently, the Death of Man. What is called for today is the Death of this World, and to do so requires cultivating a hatred for it.

8

Deleuze refutes the image of Nietzsche as a dour pessimist. Flipping that image on its head, Deleuze argues that Nietzsche is an unparalleled thinker of affirmation. But in doing so, even Deleuze's masterful pen cannot erase the many moments of negativity that impregnate Nietzsche's work. Deleuze thus turns his eye to Nietzsche's moments of creation, as exemplified in a passage from the fifty-eighth aphorism of *The Gay Science*:

> How foolish it would be to suppose that one only needs to point out the origin and this misty shroud of delusion in order to *destroy* the world that counts as real, so-called *"reality."* We can destroy only as creators.—But let us not forget: it is enough to create new names and estimations and probabilities in order to create in the long run new "things."

Dissatisfied with Nietzsche's implied goal of destruction, Deleuze inverts the phrase into "destroy in order to create" (DI, 130). This formulation appears over and again in his work. To name a few places: in *Anti-Oedipus,* Deleuze and Guattari say that capitalism destroys what came before to create its own earthly existence, a process of three tasks whereby the first is negative (destroy!) and the second two are positive (create! create!). Deleuze later argues that the painter must first destroy prior clichés before creating a new image (FB, 71–90). And in their final collaboration, Deleuze and Guattari scold "those who criticize without creating" as "the plague of philosophy" (WP, 28).

There is something disarming about the sincerity of Deleuze and Guattari's definition of philosophy as the art of constructing concepts (WP, 2). Yet it feels odd in an era full of trite invitations to being constructive: "if you don't have anything nice to say, don't say anything at all," "if constructive thoughts are planted, positive outcomes will be the result," or, simply, "be

9

constructive, not destructive." The simple if–then structure of these self-help maxims is more than logical; it discloses a transitive theory of justice. Just as the meek will inherit the earth, it promises the just deserts of construction. Good things come to those who are constructive! How far this is from Marx's "ruthless criticism of all that exists" ("Letter to Arnold Ruge"). Now that advertisers claim to be the most creative of all creatures on earth, it is time to replace creativity as the central mechanism of liberation.

Deleuze would have hated today's images of creativity—there is a great violence in comparing the fabrication of concepts to any happy means of construction; concepts are friends only to thought, as they break consensus (WP, 4–6, 99). Concepts are not discovered but the result of a catastrophe, Deleuze and Guattari say, from turning away, tiredness, distress, and distrust (6–7). True thought is rare, painful, and usually forced on us by the brutality of an event so terrible that it cannot be resolved without the difficulty of thought. As such, we must quit treating concepts as some "wonderful dowry from some wonderland" to understand the hard, rigorous work that goes into their creation (5).

Productivism is *Dark Deleuze*'s second object of criticism (connectivism being the first). It may be possible to distinguish concept creation from productivism, for the latter is "commercial professional training" that aspires for thought only beneficial "from the viewpoint of universal capitalism" (WP, 14). Maintaining such a distinction is difficult—in an age of compulsory happiness, it is easy for construction to be conflated with capitalist value, the empty promises of democracy, or just plain helpfulness (106–8). To that end, productivism distinguishes itself with two formal principles: accumulation and reproduction. First, productivism manages political conflicts through a logic of accumulation, as seen in the "full mobilizations" of

World War II as well as in Stalin's and Mao's dreary attempts to outproduce the capitalist world system. Second, productivism limits production to reproduction, as capitalism attempts to do, by initiating only those circuits of production that operate on an expanding basis (what Lenin called "imperialism"). The significance of the critique of productivism is that it expands the grammar of power beyond what is beholden to accumulation or reproduction.

Dark Deleuze does not philosophically quibble with creation. But it is easy to get drowned out by those who praise Deleuze for his "joy." The difficulty with joy is that it lies in the slippage between metaphysics and normativity. Michel Serres, for instance, remains steadfast that Deleuze's death must have been an accident because he felt that suicide was not in Deleuze's character or philosophy (Flint, "Michel Serres' Angels"). Such liberties may be authorized by the term itself, as it comes from Spinoza's *Ethics,* in which the line between the two is blurred. Joy surfaces as the feeling of pleasure that comes when a body encounters something that expands its capacities, which are affects said to "agree with my nature," to be "good" or simply "useful" (S, 239). To end the story here (though some do) would reproduce a naive hedonism based on inquiries into subjects and their self-reported affective states. Spinoza's theory of affects is not an affirmation of a subject's feelings but a proof of the inadequacy of critique. Affects are by-products emitted during the encounter that hint at a replacement for recognition or understanding as the feedback loop to indicate if knowledge was sufficient. But there are innumerable forms of knowledge, many of which invite stupidity or illusion. What characterizes Spinoza's "adequate knowledge" is its ability to create something new—it is that knowledge then becomes "identical to the construction of reality" (138). This is why Spinoza says that God = nature; knowledge-as-God is defined as that thought which increases the capacity to make actions flourish in the natural world ("I think, therefore I am active") (WP, 31). The implication is that critique is not effective in its own right, no matter how loudly it proclaims its truth. The only adequate knowledge is activity.

Deleuze corrupts the holism of an already heretical Spinoza through an old atomist proposition: the relation between two terms produces an independent third term. ("Sometimes the relations of two bodies may agree so well that they form a third relation within which the two bodies are preserved and prosper"; S, 239; H, 101). This is how Deleuze builds his metaphysics of positivity—all elements stand alone without recourse to (Hegelian) opposition, contradiction, or identity. Deleuze and Guattari's "line of flight" conceptually embodies the Nietzschean notion that things are not wholly dependent on their context of production. For them, anything that has gained its own internal consistency is free to travel outside its place of origin. They even define art this way—as impressions that have congealed enough to become their own mobile army of sensations (WP, 163–64). Deleuze and Guattari's contemporaries share this insight, most notably Foucault's strategic reversibility of power relations (*History of Sexuality*, 92–102) and Althusser's aleatory materialism (*Philosophy of the Encounter*). For Foucault, the reversibility of power is illustrated in homosexuality, which is first created as a medical category of sexual perversion but grows into a whole way of life that "spoke on its own behalf." For Althusser, the "underground current" of capitalism is made up of various noncontemporaneous elements always in a process of "becoming-necessary" that "gels at certain felicitous moments," while the singular importance of each haunting contingency simultaneously reveals the system's unstable horizon. Atomism thus shows how the world supplies the materials for its destruction.

The powers of the outside, a component of Deleuze's thought largely driven underground, offer an additional escape. First, there is this book's key pivot point: Deleuze and Guattari establish in *Anti-Oedipus* the autoproduction of the Real, which is a passive process that occurs largely beyond human understanding. Confusing metaphysics for politics, many Deleuzians parrot this production as a positive end unto itself. Yet a return to a politics worthy of the name "communism" demands the opposite, as the greatest system of autoproduction is capitalism, which throws billions into abject poverty, wages horrific wars of devastation, and subjects humanity to a growing matrix of social oppression. Appeals to the frailty of life only obscure the issue even more. To say something rather controversial, though well established by ecologists decades ago: life will survive us. All human concern for the world is ultimately selfish anthropocentrism, for it was never life that was at risk ("the combined detonation of all the world's nuclear weapons would be like a warm summer breeze to Gaia," I once heard), just the world's capacity to sustain humans (Luke, *Ecocritique*; Stengers, *In Catastrophic Times*). Second, the way forward is to invite death, not to avoid it. Deleuze and Guattari suggest this in their reworking of the death drive. Similar sentiments are echoed in the punk ethos of "no future," which paradoxically realizes that the only future we have comes when we stop reproducing the conditions of the present (Edelman, *No Future*). So let us stop romanticizing life and wish a happy death on calcified political forms, no-good solutions, and bad ways of thinking.

We must correct Deleuze's error: failing to cultivate a hatred for this world. It begins with the "ambivalent joy of hatred"—"What my soul loves, I love. What my soul hates, I hate" (F, 23; ECC, 135). Or to echo Proust, "we must be harsh, cruel, and deceptive to what we love" (P, 92). It is not even that Deleuze never mentioned hatred in a positive light; in fact, he often praises

Nietzsche's "sense of cruelty" and "taste for destruction" (DR, 53). Deleuze was too often overtaken by a naive affirmation of joy, and as such, he was unable to give hatred its necessary form. His image for the future resembles too much of the present, and those who repeat it have come to sound like a parody: "rhizomatic gardens," "cooperative self-production," and "affirming the affirmative of life." Against those maxims, the Dark Deleuze is reborn as a barbarian depicted in Rimbaud's season in hell: "I'm of a distant race: my forefathers were Scandinavian; they slashed their sides and drank their own blood. I will make cuts all over; I'll tattoo myself, I long to be as a hideous Mongol: you'll see, I'll scream in the streets. I want to be mad with rage. . . . I dreamt of crusades, of unrecorded voyages of discovery, of republics without history, wars of suppressed religion, moral revolutions, movements of races and continents" (*A Season in Hell*). Barbarian hatred is not to be indiscriminate, but it does not follow from a science of judgment. In fact, it is what is left after having done away with judgment (of God, of Man, and even of the World). Hatred is the ambivalent complement to love and, as such, can easily evade a decline into *ressentiment*. For *ressentiment* is just as much a depreciated image of love, as demonstrated by the Christian God who loved this world so much that he introduced the moral judgment of the ascetic ideal. In the end, hatred will prove to be just as important for the Death of this World as it was for the Death of God and the Death of Man.

From the Chapel to the Crypt

There are those who have hitherto only enlightened the world in various ways; the point is to darken it. Some speculate that humans first pondered the ways of the world under the brilliant light of the heavens. On that vast celestial stage, the gods played out great dramas of arts and culture. This cosmos also inspired the earliest sciences of mathematics and astronomy, which wove the many constellations into a single tapestry. As the light of the stars became cycles and then detailed calendars, so came the dawn of time.

A more modern story begins in 1609, when, upon hearing news of the Dutch invention of the telescope, Galileo created his own. Almost immediately, Galileo was peering into the dark quadrants of the moon and illustrating its angle of illumination. These discoveries would lead him to loudly endorse heliocentrism—replacing God with a new light at the center of the universe. Galileo curiously flaunts the rules of astronomy in his lunar record, as he does not date each ink wash according to its time of observation, nor does he make a photorealistic reproduction of the moon's landscape (Gingrich and van Helden, "From *Occhiale* to Printed Page," 258–62). Centuries of critics have tried to determine the source of Galileo's inaccuracy. Johannis Hevelii, the father of stenography, wondered if Galileo's instruments were too crude (*Selenographia sive Lunae Descriptio,* 205). Others suggest that he may have been too overtaken by the excitement of discovery (Kopal, *The Moon,* 225). But what if Galileo chose not to view the moon mathematically but philosophically? He was less concerned about its angles of illumination as an astronomical object than about what his telescopic *perspicillum* revealed about it as a cosmological concept. His styling of the moon reveals a way of seeing far more appropriate to baroque visual argument than to geographic measure. Galileo's ink washes demonstrate the baroque's beautiful convergences. Referring "not to an essence but rather to an operative function," Galileo's moon unfurls in the collision of multiple points of view as darkness and landscape meet in its leaping shadows (L, 3). More importantly, he marks a transition driven by "the force of divergences, impossibilities, discords, dissonances" (81). In a world no longer illuminated by the light of God, Galileo paints "many possible borders between worlds" in a chromatic scale so as to be irresolvable from the lens of any one camera set to a single angle (81). How, then, does one continue Galileo's journey to the far side of the moon? By refusing divine harmony and instead conspiring with divergent underground worlds.

The most immediate instance of lightness, connectivism, is the realization of the techno-affirmationist dream of complete transparency. The fate of such transparency is depicted in Fritz Lang's *Metropolis*. In it, the drive for complete communicability elevates transparency in the false transcendence of a New Tower of Babel. Deep in the shadows of the Lower City labors the working class, enslaved to the machines that automation promised to eliminate. Only in the catacombs does the secret rebellion commence. But instead of ending in Lang's grand Hegelian mediation, it would be better to listen to the Whore of Babylon in *Metropolis,* who says, "Let's watch the world go to hell." Such an untimely descent into darkness begins with a protest: lightness has far too long been the dominant model of thought. The road there descends from the chapel to the crypt.

Crypts are by their very nature places of seclusion. Early Christians facing public persecution fled to the underground catacombs below Rome, where they could worship in secret ("Essay upon Crypts," 73–77). Early basilicas contain crypts as a "second church" under their choirs, featuring a vaulted ceiling, many columns, several aisles, and an altar (Lübke, *Ecclesiastical Art,* 24–25). Some great churches even included a second crypt dedicated to a particular saint (26). At times, when sacred objects are of special interest, crypts of especially renowned saints have inspired mass pilgrimages (Spence-Jones, *Early Christianity and Paganism,* 269). Deleuze notes that these spaces fold in on themselves, simultaneously expressing the "autonomy of the inside" and the "independence of the façade" as an inside without an outside or an outside without an inside, depending on how you approach it (L, 28). Looking at El Greco's great baroque mannerist painting *The Burial of Count Orgaz,* we are given the choice. Above the great horizontal line, a gathering of saints ascends to the height of Jesus, whose own ascension grants the heavens eternal lightness. Below, a communion of cloaked, pale men crowd together to lay the count to rest under a dark background illuminated only by torchlight. The painting reveals the baroque truth of knowledge: "for ages there have been places where what is seen is inside: a cell, a sacristy, a crypt, a church, a theater, a study, or a print room" (L, 27–28). So beyond the association of crypts with rot and death, it is a projection of subterranean architectural power.

From the crypt, *Dark Deleuze* launches a conspiracy. It is fueled by negativity, but not one of antimonies. Following Freud, negation is not a necessary by-product of consciousness. The lesson to be drawn from him is that negation is finding a way to say "no" to those who tell us to take the world as it is. To this end, the path forward is Deleuze's nondialectical negation, the "contrary," which operates as the distance between two exclusive paths (LS, 172–80). Klossowski identifies the goal of the conspiracy as breaking the collusion between institutionalized morality, capitalism, and the state ("Circulus Vitiosus"). He then shows how Nietzsche's laughter can be used as an experimental instrument to dissolve all identities into phantasms. A number of commentators have tried to rehabilitate the conspiracy on the basis of an esoteric/exoteric distinction, whereby exoteric discourses are the mere public face to a deeper paranoia whose desire is concealed in an esoteric code. To the extent that it is true, in his book *Nietzsche and the Vicious Circle,* Klossowski warns that the esoteric tradition must be avoided because it "demystifies only in order to mystify better" (131).

The point is not to replace angelic messages with arcane ones. This raises an important question: what is an appropriately cryptic language? Deleuze and Guattari note that "the man of war brings the secret: he thinks, eats, loves, judges, arrives in secret, while the man of the state proceeds publicly" (TP, 543–44). Fortunately, in our conspiratorial world of phantasms, one does not hold a secret but instead becomes a secret. Even if she ends up spilling everything, it turns out to be nothing. Why? The secret first hides within dominant forms to limit exposure, yet what it smuggles inside is not any specific thing that needs to evade discovery. Rather, it is a perception of the secret that spreads under the shroud of secrecy: perception + secret = the secret as secretion. Conspiracies do not remain limited to a few furtive missives; their creeping insinuations are part of a universal project to permeate all of society (TP, 286–89). The best conspiracy is when it has nothing left to hide.

There is an affective dimension to our conspiracy. Pessimism becomes a necessity when writing in an era of generalized precarity, extreme class stratification, and summary executions of people of color. The trouble with the metaphysics of difference is that it does not immediately suggest a positive conception of alienation, exploitation, or social death. To the extent that those who affirm difference and its intensifications do make such violence thinkable, it appears as the consequence of deprivation. As a result, they cannot explain the simultaneous connection–separation of a body alienated from their own powers. Such joyousness makes no place for Marx's theory of exploitation in which one class systematically extracts profit by expanding the capacities of another. The conspiracy offers a way out. On the affective level, it takes the ambivalence of hatred to grasp how one's own capacities are the yoke of his oppression. On the level of strategy, it takes deep, labyrinthine paths to develop a cryptography. To do so myself, I reenact Winston's trips to the

shallow alcove of his apartment in *1984* to keep our own illic-
it diary of slogans. This is how I learned to find my own way
to say "DOWN WITH BIG BROTHER" and "If there is hope, it lies
with the proles" (181). This is because the ultimate task of *Dark
Deleuze* is but a modest one: to keep the dream of revolution
alive in counterrevolutionary times.

The conspiracy Dark Deleuze is a series of contraries.
Contraries are not poles, which are dialectical opposites that
ultimately complement each other. To distill a central argument from Deleuze's magnum opus *Difference and Repetition,*
philosophy has (to its detriment) taken the nature of thinking to
be the establishment of equivalence or logical identity between
two terms (59). As such, contrasts must avoid relating terms on
the basis of "a conceived identity, a judged analogy, an imag-
ined opposition, or a perceived similitude" (138). Deleuze sum-
marizes this argument in an interview: "It was Lévi-Strauss, I
think, who showed you had to distinguish the following two
propositions: that only similar things can differ [dialectics—
presupposing a primordial identity behind differences], and
only different things can be similar [contraries—difference pri-
mary to identity]" (N 156). There is a second reason for avoid-
ing opposites: opposites imply a "golden mean" whereby the
optimal place is found somewhere in between each extreme.
Such middling compromise is the greatest tragedy of Deleuze
and Guattari's rhetorical presentation of what appear to be
dualisms (smooth/striated, molar/molecular, arborescent/rhi-
zomatic) in *A Thousand Plateaus.* The unfortunate effect is a
legion of noncommittal commentators who preach the moder-
ation of the middle. In response, we must contaminate every
last one of those conceptual pairs with a third term that arrives
from the outside. Deleuze and Guattari set the example in how
they reimagine Dumézil's tripartite state as two opposing poles
besieged by a third term that arrives from the outside. Such a

reformulation would more closely follow Deleuze's atomism of two terms relating through the production of an independent third term. To make the stakes clear: we are told in *A Thousand Plateaus* that the state is made of two opposing poles, one liberal and one authoritarian, that in fact work in a "complementarity" not dissimilar from the dialectical logic of determinate negation—this is the model of relation that must be avoided at all costs (for more, see the section "Difference: Exclusive Disjunction, Not Inclusive Disjunction") (Dumézil, *Mitra-Varuna*). This is why *Dark Deleuze* contrasts dark to joyous and not dark to light or joyous to sad. Each contrary is a forking path, an alternate route for every instance one is tempted by affirmation.

Listed in what follows are the contrasting terms. In the column on the left, I list a series of tasks. Across each column I have placed two contrary approaches, one joyous and one dark. The association each term has to its contrary is purely incidental. Each term's contrariness is not given, as if one implied the other—I propose dark terms simply on their ability to unexpectedly usurp the operations of their contraries. Contrary approaches should be taken as mutually exclusive, as they are independent processes each meant to fulfill the given task without recourse to the other. What makes them dark is the position of exteriority from which the irregular forces of darkness attack the joy of state thought. The foreignness of relation is why each pair of contrasting terms is notably imbalanced.

My ultimate purpose is to convince readers to completely abandon all the joyous paths for their dark alternatives. The best scenario would be that these contraries fade into irrelevance after Dark Deleuze achieves its ostensible goal: the end of this world, the final defeat of the state, and full communism. It is far more likely that various aspects of darkness will be captured along the way. Like any other war machine, a dark term is defeated when it isomorphically takes on relations or forms of its joyous counterpart. So it is worth uttering a cautionary note from *A Thousand Plateaus*: even when contrary, never believe that darkness will suffice to save us.

	JOYOUS	DARK
The Task	Create Conceptions	Destroy Worlds
Subject	Assemblages	Un-becoming
Existence	Genesis	Transformation
Ontology	Realism	Materialism
Difference	Inclusive Disjunction	Exclusive Disjunction
Diagram	Complexity	Asymmetry
Organization	Rhizome	Unfolding
Ethics	Processural Democracy	Conspiratorial Communism
Affect	Intensity	Cruelty
Speed	Acceleration	Escape
Flows	Production	Interruption
Substance	Techno-Science	Political Anthropology
Nomadism	Pastoral	Barbarian
Distribution	Nomos	The Outside
Politics	Molecular	Cataclysmic
Cinema	The Forces of Bodies	The Powers of the False
The Sensible	Experience	Indiscernibility

The Extinction of Being

The Task: Destroy Worlds, Not Create Conceptions

The conspiracy against this world will be known through its war machines. A war machine is itself "a pure form of exteriority" that "explains nothing," but there are plenty of stories to tell about them (TP, 354, 427). They are the heroes of *A Thousand Plateaus*—Kleist's skull-crushing war machine, the migratory war machine that the Vandals used to sack Rome, the gun that Black Panther George Jackson grabs on the run, and the queer war machine that excretes a thousand tiny sexes. "Each time there is an operation against the state—insubordination, rioting, guerilla warfare, or revolution as an act—it can be said that a war machine has revived" (386). War machines are also the greatest villains of *A Thousand Plateaus*, making all other dangers "pale by comparison" (231)—there is the constant state appropriation of the war machine that subordinates war to its own aims (418), the folly of the commercial war machine (15), the paranoia of the fascist war machine (not the state army of totalitarianism) (230–31), and, worst of them all, the "worldwide war machine" of capitalism, "whose organization exceeds the State apparatus and passes into energy, military–industrial, and multinational complexes" to wage peace on the whole world (387, 419–21, 467).

"Make thought a war machine," Deleuze and Guattari insist. "Place thought in an immediate relation with the outside, with the forces of the outside" (TP, 376–77). Two important inventions follow: speed and secrecy. These are the affects of the war machine, its weapons of war, which "transpierce the body like arrows" (356, 394). The resulting violence is not so vulgar as to encourage blow-by-blow bloodletting or a once-and-for-all immediate killing but institutes an economy of violence whose hatred is unlimited and therefore durable. The war machine engages in war along two poles: one forms a line of destruction "prolongable to the limits of the universe," while the other draws a line of flight for the "composition of a smooth space and of the movement of people in that space" (422). Deleuze and Guattari would prefer to promote the connectivist line by saying they "make war only on the condition that they simultaneously create something else" (423). But today, that path leads to collusion with capitalism's drive toward creative destruction (Schumpeter, *Capitalism, Socialism, Democracy,* 87). This is certainly not lost on those in Silicon Valley who spread the mantra of "disruptive innovation." We can thus take heed of Deleuze and Guattari's warning against treating terms as having "an irresistible revolutionary calling" (387). It is time to accept Nietzsche's invitation to philosophize with a hammer, rendered here in the voice of Krishna: "I am become Time, the destroyer of worlds." We must find an appetite for destruction that does not betray Deleuze and Guattari's "abolitionist dream." This takes the "progressive, anxiety-ridden revelation" that destroying worlds is just another way of "smashing capitalism, of redefining socialism, of constituting a war machine capable of countering the world war machine by other means" (385, 417, 372).

Make the whole world stand still. Indeed, it may be the only way to think the present in any significant sense. To be clear: the suspension of the world is not a hunt for its conditions of reproduction or a meditative "rhapsody of sensations" (DR, 56). It is thought that treats the world as if struck by an unspecified disaster, where the best friends you have left are your own ideas. This is not the banal disaster movie, whose ambitions are usually limited to teaching us what are the bare essentials to survive. Writing the disaster is how we break free from the stifling perpetual present, for the present carries with itself a suffocating urgency. The present imposes material limits. To it, the past and the future are the empty form of time, and they must endure the complications of having a body to become part of the present (LS, 146–47, 165). The past and the future exist in their own right only through representation—the former in history as the present memorialization of things passed and the latter in the yet to come as the projection of an image of the present (147). Such re-presentation is why the future appears with the distinct impression that "we have seen it all before" (Flaxman, *Fabulation of Philosophy,* 392). The productivist sees the event of thought as an eminently practical reorientation toward the present achieved while generating a new image of the future (WP, 58). In contrast, those learning to hate the world must short-circuit the "here and now" to play out the scene differently. While still being in this world, they turn away from it. This is the life of characters so agitated that they force the world to stand still—Dostoyevsky's Idiot, the head of Kurosawa's seven samurai (TR, 317–18). Against bleating urgency that "there a fire, there's fire . . . I've got to go," they insist that everything could burn to the ground but nothing happens, because one must seek out a more urgent problem!

There are those who say that we already have one foot in utopia; but would it not be more suitable to say that we have both feet firmly planted in a present slouching toward dystopia? Deleuze and Guattari call on utopia in their search for a new people and a new earth (WP, 99). They look to Samuel

Butler, dissecting his *Erewhon* as a simultaneous "now-here" and "no-where" (100). Yet a closer examination of his novel reveals utopia to be a farce. While not exactly a dystopia, the utopia Erewhon is a comic satire of the British Empire. The narrator is a crass traveler with settler colonial dreams who catalogs the strange ways of Erewhon—in chapters 10 and 11, he outlines how they punish the sick ("convicted of aggravated bronchitis") and sentence the misfortunate to hard labor ("ill luck of any kind . . . is considered an offense against society") but nurture financial transgressions with medicine ("taken to a hospital and most carefully tended at the public expense"). Beyond being an object lesson in reading footnotes, Deleuze and Guattari's reference to *Erewhon* demands an attention to the exact configuration of conceptual devices (*dispositifs*) and how power flows through them. Link thought with its epoch, they suggest, begin with a survey to identify whatever forces are already circulating and then work with them—"connecting up with what is real here and now in the struggle against capitalism, relaunching new struggles whenever the earlier one is betrayed" (100). They warn of "proud affirmation" as the guise of restoration that opens the door to transcendence, such as appeals to truth, right, or authority (100). For Butler, *Erewhon* summons neither a new people nor a new earth but is instead a field guide to negate everything he finds intolerable in his present. Utopia becomes the map to transform the now-here into the no-where.

"It should have been an apocalyptic book," laments Deleuze, disappointed that the "old style" *Difference and Repetition* did not make apparent a key implication—he killed God, humankind, and even the world (xxi). The Death of God began long before Deleuze, who sees Feuerbach as completing it long before Nietzsche with the proposition that "since man has never been anything but the unfold of man, man must fold and refold God" (F, 130). Nietzsche identifies a different problem: that God was reborn in the form of Man. For Deleuze, it takes Foucault to establish the finitude of humanity—"Man has not always existed, and will not exist forever"—thus sealing its fate (F, 124). But to destroy the world . . . that is the truly heretical proposition. A small group of dissident Deleuze scholars have rallied around the slogan that "there is no 'ontology of Deleuze'"—Gregory Flaxman, Anne Sauvagnargues, Gregg Lambert, and François Zourabichvili, to name a few (Zourabichvili, *A Philosophy of the Event*, 36). The statement does not imply that ontology is an illusion, but criticizing those who build a Deleuzian system around a coherent ontology of the world is ill considered, as it fails draw a line to the outside—"to incalculable forces, to chance and improvisation, to the future" (Flaxman, "Politics and Ontology"). Blazing such a path may require "the extinction of the term 'being' and therefore of ontology," or in so many words, a destruction of this world (37). Deleuze and Guattari suggest as much when they propose to "overthrow ontology" (TP, 25). Summed up, this stance names the "joyful pessimist" Deleuze. Too restless to stop there, the Dark Deleuze broadens the *coup de force* into a fierce pessimism that shatters the cosmos.

The Subject: Un-becoming, Not Assemblages

Subjectivity is shameful—"subjects are born quite as much from misery as from triumph" (N, 151). It grows from the seeds of a "composite feeling" made from the compromises with our time: the shame of being alive, the shame of indignity, the shame that it happens to others, the shame that others can do it, and the shame of not being able to prevent it (WP, 108, 225). Existence is the result of a disaster, yet it says very little about us; it does not explain but rather must be explained. This is what makes shame "one of philosophy's most powerful motifs" (108). The subject is always something derivative that "comes into being and vanishes in the fabric of what one says, what one sees," resembling "specks dancing in the dust of the visible and permutations in an anonymous babble" (N, 108). This does not keep some from clinging to their shame. On this account, Deleuze has nothing but scorn for identity politics—"we have to counter people who think 'I'm this, I'm that' . . . arguments from one's own privileged experience are bad and reactionary arguments" (N, 11–12). Shame is our defense against these people, queer theorists remind us, and it must be put to work on them as a weapon—an affect that acts as a solvent to dissolve whatever binds it to an identity (Halperin and Traub, "Beyond Gay Pride," 25). There are those who have worked to square identity with Deleuze (Donna Haraway, Tim Dean, Jasbir Puar, Édouard Glissant). Their theorizations only avoid the problem of shame to the extent that they make identity's many perforations into points of leverage and transformed differences into a million cutting edges.

For some, the world is made up of assemblages, and all assemblages are subjects. In no time, people, hurricanes, and battles all get addressed in the same register (as all subjects should be afforded proper names)! Although this is, perhaps, technically true, such assemblage-thinking misses the point—it reduces subjectivity to the name we use to pin down the sum of a body's capacities (AT, 256–57). It sanctifies a bloodless world by cataloging the networks that make up its many attributes. This is why assemblage-modeling is a perfect fit in a world where capitalism produces subjectivity "the same way it produces Prell shampoo or Ford cars" (AO, 245). Further proof of its noxious conservativsm is arch-thinkers Manuel DeLanda's and Bruno Latour's dismissive rejection of Marxism. Fortunately, Deleuze already warned us by channeling Spinoza on the limits of adequate knowledge, in the often-repeated words that "we do not know what a body is capable of" (NP, 39). The phrase should not be read as an appeal to some evasive essence but simply as applying a principle of Deleuze's transcendental empiricism, which holds that the conditions of actual experience are not represented through empirical tracing (DR, 95, 221, 321). This is crucial, because philosophy is too easily thrown back into the transcendental illusions through the personal identitarian experiences built by self-centered habits of mind (DR, 207–8, 73, 119). The pitfall of run-of-the-mill empiricists is that even in the best-case scenario, when they step out of the perspective of the subject, they still reduce existence to conditions of reproduction or chart something's "degree of freedom." For us, then, the subject should be spoken about scornfully as simply the sum of a body's habits, most of which are marshaled to evade thought.

The undoing of the subject is un-becoming. Deleuze withholds praise for the subject but does not deny it a place, unlike Althusser, who theorizes "subjectivity without a subject" (Badiou, "Althusser," 58–67). But subjects are only interesting when they cast a "line to the outside"—in short, when they stop being subjects (with a double emphasis on "being" and "subjects") (N, 99). This process is how Deleuze describes Foucault's subjectivization, which is not a "coming back" to subjectivity to rescue it but the disintegration of the subject as it evaporates into a field of forces where neither persons nor identities survive (N, 93). This is the secret to becoming, for it has nothing to do with "subjects developing into more of themselves." Becoming is really a process of un-becoming. In what Elizabeth Grosz calls "undoing the givenness of the given" of *Becoming Undone,* un-becoming exercises undoing, a process that works to "undo the stabilities of identity, knowledge, location, and being" (210, 3). But in proposing undoing as an alternative to subjectivity, it is necessary to be specific about how to orient the process. While it is easy for an aesthete to indulge in the powers of the outside like a good after-dinner drink, "letting loose, freeing up, and putting into play," undoing can fulfill the higher purpose of nursing a hatred for this world (55). For it is only when we locate something intolerable outside ourselves that we will "leap beyond shame" and "transform [our] paltry undertakings into a war of resistance and liberation" (ECC, 125).

Existence: Transformation, Not Genesis

Philosophy "has always maintained an essential relation to the law, the institution, and the contract" (DI, 259). Foundations thus hold a special place in philosophy, with philosophers obsessively writing and rewriting the book of Genesis. It is Kant, the great thinker of the genetic "condition," "who finally turns the philosopher into the Judge at the same time that reason becomes a tribunal" (WP, 72). Deleuze refuses to disown his own "in the beginning." But for him, the movement of thought follows an explosive line whose genesis comprises problems manifest from imperceptible forces that disrupt habits of mind. Such thinking does not build a courthouse of reason whereby each advance in thought confirms more about what was already self-evident, as if developing an elaborate mirror of the world (N 38–39; DR 129). In contrast, the "enemy" Kant does something intolerable by creating a theory of law that diverts the ungrounding called thought, ending its journey to an unrecognized *terra incognita* (DI 58; DR 136). He does this by reversing the Greeks, making it so the law does not depend on the good like a material substrate and instead deriving the good from law—"the good is that which the law expresses when it expresses itself" (K, 43). Expressing their disapproval, Deleuze and Guattari draw a "portrait" of Kant that depicts him as a vampiric death machine feeding off the world (WP, 56). But even as Kant makes the law rational, he opens up a way out in the third critique through a synthesis that allows a free harmony of the faculties, though he is quick to betray it (WP, 32, 46, 100). Latching on to this furtive insight, Deleuze advances a "mobile war machine" in its place, to be used against the "rational administrative machine" of philosophers who "would be the bureaucrats of pure reason" (DI, 259). And in making thought into a siege engine, it gains the nomadic force of transformation. The key is to avoid founding a new order on a new image of world. Fortunately, we can follow the pure idea of Toynbee's nomads who shed their habits so they do not have to leave their habitats.

Ontology: Materialism, Not Realism

Our appetite produces the real. But do not mistake the real for a simple projection—it is real through and through. "I take my desires for reality because I believe in the reality of my desire," says the streets of Paris in 1968 (Anonymous, "Graffiti"). In response, Deleuze and Guattari say that "the real is not impossible, on the contrary, within the real everything is possible, everything becomes possible" (AO, 27). The only reason that we lack anything, they say, is that our social system deprives us of what we desire. On this account, our taste is not a correlationist yearning, as Quentin Meillassoux calls it in *After Finitude,* which would say that we are reaching for a thing-in-itself always outside the grasp of our perception. Yet this should not lead us to embrace the philosophical realism that connectivists apologize for as an attack on anthropocentrism. "Things exist independently of perception," the realists assert to bring the Death of Man. But they forget that "there is no such thing as either man or nature" when there is "simply the production of production itself" (AO, 2). So while there is no man, nature also must vanish. Without treating the real as truly artificial, thought is regrounded as a theology of this world that plugs all the leaks to the outside.

A superior materialism "constructs a real that is yet to come" (TP, 142). It does not follow so-called new materialism, which is really just a new form of animism, but Marxist materialism as the revolutionary subversion of material necessity. Deleuze and Guattari find their superior materialism by exchanging the theater of representation for the factory of production. It is the materialism of Epicurus and the atomism of the swerve as the necessity of contingency (Althusser, *Philosophy of the Encounter*, 174). This permanent revocation of the fait accompli is at work in politics of destruction, which has too long been mistaken for deliberation but is instead exemplified by the war machines of popular insurrection whose success is registered by the streets themselves—consider the words of the Invisible Committee in *To Our Friends*: "Like any specific strike, it is a politics of the accomplished fact. It is the reign of the initiative, of practical complicity, of gesture. As to decision, it accomplishes that in the streets, reminding those who've forgotten, that 'popular' comes from the Latin *populor,* 'to ravage, devastate.' It is a fullness of expression . . . and a nullity of deliberation" (54). By showing the nondurability of what is taken as real, so-called reality itself, communist politics is a conspiracy that writes the destruction of the world.

Difference: Exclusive Disjunction, Not Inclusive Disjunction

"Too much!" is a potential rallying cry—too many products, too many choices, too much of this world! Instead, become contrary! Difference, for Deleuze, is the result of a "disjunctive synthesis" that produces a series of "disjointed and divergent" differences (LS, 174–76, 177–80). Importantly, these differences can be immediately brought together at a distance through resonance, globally coordinated, or contracted into a divergent multitude (172–76). Following the rule "always perversify," Deleuze and Guattari propose including disjunctions in a mad mixture of "world-historical, political, and racial content" as a strategy for scrambling oppressive codes (AO, 15, 88–89).

Global capitalism quickly caught on. Michael Hardt and Antonio Negri have shown us how it rules over a virtual Empire of difference that eagerly coordinates a wide arrangement of diverging differences while also producing many more of its own (*Empire*, 44–45, 138–56, 190–201, 339–43). Capital is now indistinguishable from the exemplary subject, the schizo, who is voiced by Nietzsche in his wild claims to be "all the names of history" (AO, 86)! Power is now diffuse, and the antagonism of Marx's class war has been drowned in an overwhelming sea of difference. This development calls for a reorientation that entails learning how to *become contrary*. In the case of Dark Deleuze, the contrarian position is the forced choice of "this, not that." Deleuze is perfectly happy to demand "no possible compromise between Hegel and Nietzsche" (NP, 195). Why not experiment with our own exclusive disjunctive synthesis that is limited, restrictive, and constrained? Hardt and Negri take their cue from those in the Global South who "homogenize real differences" to name "the potential unity of an international opposition, the confluence of anticapitalist countries and forces" (*Empire*, 334). A better response has been the terrifying screams of no that occasionally break apart its grand accords (Holloway, "The Scream," 1). Though not demanding the suppression of difference, the problem of Empire reignites the necessity of conspiracy, the power of hatred, and the task of destroying worlds.

Advancing toward Nothing

Diagram: Asymmetry, Not Complexity

"The 'nothing' (Heidegger), the 'trace' or 'différance' (Derrida), the 'surplus always exterior to the totality' (Levinas), the 'differend' (Lyotard), 'the invisible' (Althusser)," and "the 'pariah' (Arendt), 'the jew' (Lyotard), the 'migrant' (Virilio), the 'nomad' (Deleuze and Guattari), the 'hybrid' (Bhabha), the 'catachrestic remainder' (Spivak), the 'non-being' (Dussel), the 'refugee' (Agamben), and, most resonantly, the 'émigré' (Said)," are the terms literary theorist William Spanos uses to describe the fleeting figures of the late twentieth century ("Question of Philosophy," 173). Each term names a conflict between differences in kind, mapping lines of flight to the outside and those who dwell there. They speak of effects not equal to their cause. The generic term for this relation is *asymmetry,* which expresses difference as formal inequivalence. Asymmetry works to impede reciprocal relations and prevent reversibility. It diagrammatically starts by constituting two formally distinct terms as contrary asymmetry. It is maintained by concretely establishing a relationship of incommensurability between their sets of forces.

Complexity is snake oil in the age of singularity—everyone and everything is a unique snowflake, what relations they can establish is not predetermined, and what they can become is limited most by how well they apply themselves! Any criticism of complexity must take into account its three levels: complexity as a fact, complexity as a resource, and complexity as deferral. As a fact, it culminates in a "flat ontology" that stitches together difference into a strange alliance of philosophy and science (Delanda, *Intensive Science,* 46–47). Though offering some provocative insights, this flattening still often leads to "a uniformization of diversity" and "equalization of inequality" (DR, 223). As a resource, the labyrinthine structure of complex systems can both mobilize and impair forces. Such complexity multiplies paths, which stocks one's arsenal with either a range of new options (as in de Certeau's "tactics") or a trap to bog down their opponents (Kafka's *The Trial*). It is this second aspect that contributes to the third dimension of complexity: deferral. A matter's "complexity" has become a way to defer a sufficient answer ("it is too complex for me to give a complete answer now . . ."). The trouble with deferral is its collusion with capitalist time, which delays the arrival of the proletarian revolution (Balibar, *Philosophy of Marx,* 101). Just ask complexity progenitor Stuart Kauffman, who now speaks in a mixture of religious mysticism and computational entrepreneurship (*Reinventing the Sacred*; Kauffman et al., "Economic Opportunity").

Deleuze outlines his case for asymmetry in *Difference and Repetition*. Everything we know is the work of a calculating god whose numbers fail to add up, he says (DR, 222). The effect is a basic injustice, an "irreducible inequality," that is "the world" (222). "If the calculations were exact there would be no world," Deleuze argues, that makes the world itself the "remainder" that is "the real in the world understood in terms of fractional or even incommensurable numbers" (222). This asymmetry is not meant as a refutation of the dubious hypothesis of the computational universe, though he does thoroughly show how the "partial truth" of energetics (e.g., the thermodynamics of entropy) is a "transcendental physical illusion" that should not be applied to the rest of the world (225, 229). The wider significance of asymmetry is an alternative to dialectics. A dialectical framing of gender, for instance, would establish an intrinsic relation between masculinity and femininity, hopelessly entangling each within each other. Extracted from dialectics, Alexander Galloway and Eugene Thacker note in their media theory of the exploit that "it is not simply that feminism is opposed to patriarchy, but that they are asymmetrically opposed; racism and antiracism are not just opposed but exist in a relationship of asymmetry" (*The Exploit*, 14). The result is a formal mechanism for political antagonism that draws on the powers of the outside.

Asymmetry is ultimately a question of combat, even if it is formally established diagrammatically. Its best realization was the twentieth-century guerrilla. The guerilla demonstrates two things about asymmetry: first, each side is opposed in terms of its strategic imperatives, but second, as each side varies in orientation, it also varies in type. As Henry Kissinger writes about the American strategy in "The Vietnam Negotiations" for *Foreign Affairs,*

> we fought a military war; our opponents fought a political one. We sought physical attrition; our opponents aimed for our psychological exhaustion. In the process we lost sight of one of the cardinal maxims of guerrilla war: the guerrilla wins if he does not lose. The conventional army loses if it does not win. The North Vietnamese used their armed forces the way a bull-fighter uses his cape—to keep us lunging in areas of marginal political importance. (214)

Fact: while the United States was fighting a war, Vietnam was engaged in combat; one for domination, the other for freedom (ECC, 132–35). This is how Marxist struggles for national liberation raised formal asymmetry as a resource for world-historical proportions. Mao defeated the national army of China with guerrillas who "move amongst the people as a fish swims in the sea." Che helped Castro's rebels flood the countryside so that they could spark a revolution that would eventually consume the cities. We must find ways to avoid complexity from deferring our own "full guerrilla warfare" (LS, 156–57).

Affect: Cruelty, Not Intensity

The story of a tyrant: finding his cruelty mollified, God burdens the world with infinite debt. Before him, memories were written on the body in a "terrible alphabet" so as never to forget them (AO, 145). This system was cruel but finite, which allowed it to form elaborate crisscrossing systems that warded off the centralization of power, such as potlatches (190). A paranoid despot arrives from the outside, as described by Nietzsche in *On the Genealogy of Morality,* installing history "just like lightning appears, too terrible, sudden," with the founding of the state to redirect the horizontal lines of alliance up and toward himself. Finite is made infinite—"everything is owed to the king" (AO, 192). Against the infinite torture of unlimited debt, cruelty combats both history and the judgment of God with "a writing of blood and life that is opposed to the writing of the book" (ECC, 128). Cruelty returns as language written on flesh—"terrible signs that lacerate bodies and stain them" as "the incisions and pigments" that reveal "what they owe and are owed" (AO, 128). Only then does the eternal collapse into the finitude of our existence.

Ours is "the most cruel of all worlds" (DI, 108). Cruelty has a lighter cousin, intensity, which induces the event of individuation that "affirms difference" without resorting to extension's depth (DR, 233). The definition of intensity as "felt" has been the source of incredible confusion. Having reduced intensity to a special kind of feeling, practitioners of "affect studies" perform autoethnographies of the ineffable. This is quite peculiar given the antiphenomenology of Deleuze's transcendental empiricism, which is explicitly nonhuman, prepersonal, and asubjective. Instead of intensity as "a strong feeling," cruelty more aptly describes the "being of the sensible" as "the demons, the sign-bearers," who bring thought to us (266). Consider how Deleuze's *Difference and Repetition* opens with lightning streaking through the black sky and ends with all the drops of the world swelling into a single ocean of excess (28, 304). Toward the end, he tells us that history presides over every determination since the birth of the world (219). Even though it may not progress "by its bad side," as Marx would have it through his critique of Proudhon, history is not "any less bloody or cruel as a result" (268).

Artaud's Theater of Cruelty gives shape to the way forward. He would be amused by the cinematic experiment of *A Clockwork Orange*. His theatrical cruelty targets those who see themselves as Alex—those who complain, "I can no longer think what I want, the moving images-are-substituted for my own thoughts" (C2, 166). The resulting theater is not for telling stories but to "empower," to implant images in the brains of those powerless to stop it (174, 166). The cruel force of these images strikes something in the skull but not the mind (a nerve? brain matter?) (167). But the only thought it allows us to ponder is *the fact that we are not yet thinking*, that we are "powerless to think the whole and to think oneself," a "thought which is always fossilized, dislocated, collapsed" (167). Cruelty here is "a dissociative force," "a figure of nothingness," and "a hole in appearance" good only for unlinking us from ourselves (167).

Organization: Unfolding, Not Rhizome

Enough with rhizomes. Although they were a suggestive image of thought thirty-five years ago, our present is dominated by the Cold War technology of the Internet that was made as a rhizomatic network for surviving nuclear war. The rhizome was a convincing snapshot of things to come, but Deleuze and Guattari left out a few things, most notably the question of movement. How does a rhizome advance, except in the crawl of the blob that slowly takes over everything? This is probably why connectivists have come to revere it—the alleged open ecology of the network specifies nothing except the bluster of its own inevitability. We know better than to think that a rhizome is enough to save us. Even something as rhizomatic as the Internet is still governed by a set of decentralized protocols that helps it maintain its consistency—the drawback being that these forms of control are diffuse, not immediately apparent, and difficult to resist (Galloway, *Protocol*, 61–72).

A contrary path: cast a line to the outside! These lines are found in folds, which are what connects a world where "relations are external to their terms" (H, 101). It is through the external bridge of the fold that "a world where terms exist like veritable atoms" communicates through their irreducible exteriority (DI, 163). More importantly, folding is movement. The inside is not erased from this world; rather, the interior is an operation of the outside (F, 97). Such "in-folding" is a structuration, "the folding back on itself of the fiber to form a compact structure" that transforms mere sedimentation into hardened strata (TP, 42). It is in this way that we can understand folding as a double-relation of force enveloping itself (and not of some forces' relation to others) as found in inorganic life, biological evolution, art, and thought (N, 92). But folding only accounts for one moment in the rhythm of movement; it is complemented by unfolding—"to unfold is to increase to grow; whereas to fold is to diminish, to reduce, 'to withdraw into the recesses of a world'" (L, 8–9).

Although called joyous by some, the great unfolding sparks an experience of terror driven by the question, "how far can we unfold the line without falling into a breathless void, into death, and how can we fold it, but without losing touch with it, to produce an inside copresent with the outside, corresponding to the outside?" (N, 113). A boring biological example is an animal's deterritorialization of its milieu by infolding a function by way of an organ that enables it to escape to form new relations with a new outside, such as a tetrapod's water retrainment, which enabled it to carry the sea with it on land. The most exciting version of unfolding operates purely in time. As a narrative device, unfolding builds tension until it suddenly "bursts open like a spring" (N, 151). Expectation, anticipation, climax, release. *Modern Times* is a masterful piece of unfolding. At a certain point ("the moment Charlie Chaplin makes the board fall on his head for a second time"), the film unfolds with the "short-circuits of a disconnected piece of machinery" (AO, 317). We cease to identify with the main character and instead envelop his events, surprises, premonitions, and habits. There is no more to unfold at dawn as the couple, "seen from the back, all black, whose shadows are not projected by any sun, advance toward nothing" (317). A line of telegraph poles on the left and pathetic trees on the right, the two fade into an empty road with no horizon—disappearing as they unfold into the void.

Unfolding operates through conduction, not communication—at least according to Jean-François Lyotard in *Libidinal Economy* (254–62). As a conductor of affects, unfolding does not build capacities through the accumulative logic of rhizomes, which changes through addition or subtraction.

Unfolding's disconnection is not the dampening of power but the buildup of charges that jump across the divide. This operation is so vital that Deleuze elevates unfolding to the absolute of unfolding substance itself (S, 310). Yet this process always takes place through a body, which stands at the limit of wild unfolding. The body staves off the "operation of vertigo" that comes from chasing after the "tiny and moving folds that waft me along at excessive speed" (L, 93). Seen from its slower speed, we see that unfolding generates force. Consider Lyotard's project of an "invulnerable conspiracy, headless, homeless, with neither programme nor project," which begins by "deploying a thousand cancerous tensors" (262) across the body's "great ephemeral skin":

Open the so-called body and spread out all its surfaces: not only the skin with each of its folds, wrinkles, scars, with its great velvety planes, and contiguous to that, the scalp and its mane of hair, the tender pubic fur, nipples, hair, hard transparent skin under the heel, the light frills of the eyelids, set with lashes—but open and spread, expose the labia majora, so also the labia minora with their blue network bathed in mucus, dilate the diaphragm of the anal sphincter, longitudinally cut and flatten out the black conduit of the rectum, then the colon, then the caecum, now a ribbon with its surface all striated and polluted with shit; as though your dressmaker's scissors were opening the leg of an old pair of trousers, go on, expose the small intestines' alleged interior, the jejunum, the ileum, the duodenum, or else, at the other end, undo the mouth at its comers, pull out the tongue at its most distant roots and split it. Spread out the bats' wings of the palate and its damp basements, open the trachea and make it the skeleton of a boat under construction; armed with scalpels and tweezers, dismantle and lay out the bundles and bodies of the encephalon; and then the whole network of veins and arteries, intact, on an immense mattress, and then the lymphatic network, and the fine bony pieces of the wrist, the ankle, take them apart and put them end to end with all the layers of nerve tissue which surround the aqueous humours and the cavernous body of the penis, and extract the great muscles, the great dorsal nets, spread them out like smooth sleeping dolphins. (1–2)

Though Lyotard's account is compelling, we must remain more vigilant. For what is it that fuels capitalism if not the massive energy generated through the unfolding of bodies? This is what inspires the famous line of *The Manifesto of the Communist Party*, whereby the constant revolutionizing of the forces of production leads to an "uninterrupted disturbance of all social conditions, everlasting uncertainty and agitation" summarized in the phrase "all that is solid melts into air" (chapter 1). But to be clear: communism is revolutionary because it too believes in the process of dissolution. Capitalism is to be criticized for falling short—it pairs the conductive power of unfolding with the rhizomatic logic of accumulation. A communism worthy of its name pushes unfolding to its limit.

Ethics: Conspiratorial Communism, Not Processual Democracy

Democracy should be abolished. Spinozist champions of democracy, such as Antonio Negri, consider Deleuze a fellow traveler. Some Deleuzians have even tried to smuggle democracy back into his metaphysics, some even pervert him into a liberal. Yet Deleuze lumps nothing but hatred upon democracy—summarized by his mocking of the phrases "Everything is equal!" and "Everything returns!" at the beginning and end of *Difference and Repetition*. Against the principle of equivalence implied in the first, he agrees with Nietzsche, who criticizes contract, consensus, and communication. Against the principle of continuity implied in the second, he agrees with Marx, who rejects the liberal proceduralism that underwrites rights as an obfuscation of power. More than enough ink has been spilled to support both of these positions. But to get the tenor pitch perfect, it is worth mentioning that Deleuze and Guattari viciously criticize democracy in their collaborations, usually by calling it the cousin of totalitarianism. They discuss democracy, fascism, and socialism as all related in *Anti-Oedipus* (261). In *A Thousand Plateaus,* they discuss "military democracy" (394), "social democracy" as the complementary pole of the State to "totalitarianism" (462), "totalitarian-social democracy" (463), and a poverty-stricken "Third World social democracy" (468). In *What Is Philosophy?,* they speak of Athenian "colonizing democracy" (97), hegemonic democracy (98), democracy being caught up with dictatorial states (106), a social democracy that "has given the order to fire when the poor come out of their territory or ghetto" (107), and a Nazi democracy (108), which all lead them to conclude that their utopian "new people and a new earth . . . will not be found in our democracies" (108). Together, they can be neatly summarized: no matter how perfect, democracy always relies on a transcendent sovereign judgment backed by the threat of force. Only twice is Deleuze caught with his pants down in regard to democracy, both in moments of pandering—once in a letter to Antonio Negri's jailers that appeals through self-distance to "everyone committed to democracy," and again when discussing America's "virile and popular loves" in a brief paean to Walt Whitman (TR, 169; ECC, 60). All other "democratic" Deleuzes are the inventions of his commentators.

Deleuze happily embraces a Marxism so anti-State that it refuses the project of democracy. It is up to us to render his Marxism in darker terms than Rancière, who would rather break down the state through the democratic dissensus of *aesthesis* acting as "the power of an ontological difference between two orders of reality" (*Dissensus,* 180). Outright, darkness begins by subverting

Negri's joyous celebration of democracy, which offers a productivist composition of forces as both the conditions of and resolution to capitalism (Ruddick, "Politics of Affect"). If Negriism was true, the only thing left for us to do is to "dump the bosses off our backs" (Hardt, "Common in Communism"). But the balance of power is far too ambivalent to make the epochal declaration that a revolutionary subject, such as the multitude, has already been produced and merely needs to be found. Our mad black communism is not a reworking of Marx's universalism, which is the seamless unity of thought and action that can be found in productivist appeals to immanence as immediate and unmediated, that is to say, automatic (PI, 29; DR, 29). On this account, an a priori communism is too dangerously close to Kant (DI, 60). We have no use for the judgment of a communist *natura,* which comes from the Joyous Deleuzians' confusion of metaphysics for politics. Neither automatic or automated, our communism is not tempted by the fully automated luxury communism of cybernetics, which is a temptation only from the perspective of control societies. Our communism is nothing but the conspiracy of communism (against ontology). It is the conspiracy to destroy the factory of production. As a conspiracy, communism is a war machine that turns the autoproductive processes of the Real into weapons for destroying any project built on metaphysical consistency. It targets the collusion between the creation of concepts and the reproduction of this world. In this sense, it wages a guerilla struggle against those who joyfully affirm "the ontology of Deleuze." It is a conspiracy for at least two reasons: first, it has a penchant for negativity that makes its revolutionary force appear as a conspiracy against everything that the joyful take as a given; second, its inclination toward collective forms of asymmetric struggle sets it wholly at odds with scholarly common sense. It dares any communism worth its name to wage a war of annihilation against God, Man, and the World itself.

Breakdown, Destruction, Ruin

Speed: Escape, Not Acceleration

Deleuze and Guattari's "accelerationism" has been too tarnished to rehabilitate. The idea was hatched by Nick Land, who held a charismatic influence over the students of the Cybernetic Culture Research Unit at the University of Warwick during the late 1990s. Drawing from Deleuze and Guattari's insistence on "accelerating the process" of capitalist deterritorialization to make a revolutionary breakthrough, Land instead suggests that the commodity system "attains its own 'angular momentum'" to become a one-way street impervious to interventions, as it is made up of cosmic-scale processes that are largely blind to human cultural inputs (*Thirst for Annihilation*, 80). For him, the accelerating speed of capital has only one possible conclusion: "a run-away whirlwind of dissolution, whose hub is the virtual zero of impersonal metropolitan accumulation" that hurls the human animal "into a new nakedness, as everything stable is progressively liquidated in the storm" (80). When he initially wrote this position, he left its significance open-ended, only later cashing it out through a neoreactionary project called the "Dark Enlightenment." Land explains that the project is dark because he eagerly adopts a "scary" mixture of cognitive elitism, racist social Darwinism, and autocratic Austrian economics. He denounces leftists as theologians of "the Cathedral" founded at "Grievance Studies departments of New England universities," whose appeals to antiracism, democracy, and equality are a type of authoritarian theology.

Commenting later on Williams and Srnicek's "#Accelerate Manifesto for an Accelerationist Politics," Land gleefully accuses those leftists who speak favorably about capital's destructive forces as "conditional accelerationists" ("Annotated #Accelerate (#3)"). He says that they can only distinguish their position from his own by way of an empty moralism in no position to direct the process. There is perhaps some truth to Land's criticism of so-called Left Accelerationism as far as they endorse Maoist skepticism for tradition and enthusiasm for productive forces, a social democratic project for a new hegemony, or an intellectual mission of "new rationalism"—all of which seek to mitigate capitalism's destructive tendencies without outlining real steps to actualize its own future. To substantiate his case, Land argues that "within capitalist futures markets, the non-actual has effective currency," which makes it "not an 'imaginary' but an integral part of the virtual body of capital" because it is "an operationalized realization of the future," so "while capital has an increasingly densely-realized future, its leftist enemies have only a manifestly pretend one" ("Annotated #Accelerate (#2b)"). The trouble then with either accelerationism is that *neither takes the process far enough,* which is to say, all accelerationism is conditional because it fails to surrender to the outside. As such, Land dresses his fascism up as an athleticism to hide the cowardice of defending the forces of this world, namely, the courthouse of reason, the authority of the market, and a religious faith in technology.

A truly dark path undoes everything that makes up this world. Deleuze and Guattari's proposal to "accelerate the process" follows from R. D. Laing's clinical prescription for more madness in our "veritable age of Darkness" (AO, 131). He supports the mad in turning "the destruction wrecked on them" into a force of dissolution against the "alienated starting point" of normality. This is a method made for breaking with the inside, which "turns in on itself" when "pierced by a hole, a lake, a flame, a tornado, an explosion," so that the outside comes flooding in (132). Such a break can go one of two ways: it can be a breakdown or a breakthrough (239, 132).

The best "breakthrough" is "making a break for it." Deleuze is fond of repeating Black Panther George Jackson, who writes from prison that "yes, I can very well escape, but during my escape, I'm looking for a weapon" (DI, 277). The phrase applies to far more than Jackson's literal imprisonment in San Quentin— what he really wanted was liberation from the American capitalist system of racial oppression, which is truly what killed him during his final escape attempt (eleven years into his one-year-to-life indefinite sentence for robbing a gas station for $70). The necessity of weapons should be clear. Even the most terrifying nomadic war machine is overshadowed by the state, which calls its operations "keeping the peace" (as documented by Foucault in his "Society Must Be Defended" lectures and beyond). Such violence has renewed meaning in 2015 as I write in the wake of a white supremacist massacre and as an outcry about racist police violence has finally started to generalize. Jackson stands as a reminder that a revolutionary line of flight must remain active; revolution is not a system-effect, though capitalism as a "system leaking all over the place" establishes the terrain for "revolutionary escape" (such as a propaganda system that can be infiltrated to attract outside conspirators or a legal system that provides lawyers who can smuggle subversive objects into controlled spaces) (DI, 270). The brilliant guerilla Che wrote the steps for one such dance, the minuet:

the guerrillas begin by encircling an advancing column and splitting into a number of "points," each with enough distance to avoid themselves being encircled; a couple pairs off and begins their dance as one of the guerrilla points attacks and draws out the enemy, after which they fall back and a different point attacks—the goal is not annihilation but to immobilize to the point of fatigue (Guevara, *Guerilla Warfare*, 58–59).

Escapism is the great betrayer of escape. The former is simply "withdrawing from the social," whereas the latter learns to "eat away at [the social] and penetrate it," everywhere setting up "charges that will explode what will explore, make fall what must fall, make escape what must escape" as a "revolutionary force" (AO, 341). The same distinction also holds between two models of autonomy: temporary autonomous zones and zones of offensive opacity. Temporary autonomous zones are momentary bursts of carnivalesque energy that proponent Hakim Bey says "vanish, leaving behind it an empty husk" when the forces of definition arrive (*Temporary Autonomous Zone*, 100). Deleuze and Guattari suggest, contrary to orthodox Marxists, that societies are defined by how they manage their paths of escape (rather than their modes of production) (TP, 435). As such, "psychotopological" distance established by temporary autonomous zones does not create a significant enough rupture to open into anything else and thus collapses escape into escape-ism. Tiqqun's zones of offensive opacity are an improvement, as they oppose a wider web of cybernetic governance without packing maximum intensity into a single moment (Anonymous, "De l'Hypothèse Cybernétique," 334–38). Opacity is its first principle, something they learn from the long tradition of autonomists and anarchists whose most militant factions would refuse all engagement with parliamentary politics, labor and unions, and news media. Offensive orientation is its second principle, though tempered by the famous line from *The Internationale,* "la crosse en l'air," with the butts of our guns held high in the air: knowing we can take the fight to the trenches, or even take power, but refuse it anyway. Tiqqun is well aware of the difficult history behind the state assassinations of the Black Panther Party and the Red Army Faction, so they know to resist militarization lest they become an army or be liquidated. The advantage of this "strategic withdrawal" is autonomy, especially as communism becomes its qualitative guide. Posing communism as oppositional self-determination, it takes the whole social apparatus of capture as its contrary—against any temptation to engage the social, for whatever resources offered, arises a demand to be met by a parallel space of communism.

Flows: Interruption, Not Production

The schizo is dead! Long live the schizo! Schizo culture appealed to a society seized by postwar consumer boredom. "Can't we produce something other than toasters and cars? How about free speech, free school, free love, free verse!" It is no exaggeration to say that the events of May 1968 were sparked by a Situationist intolerance for boredom ("boredom is always counter-revolutionary," says Guy Debord; "Bad Old Days Will End," 36). In the time since the 1972 publication of *Anti-Oedipus,* capitalism has embraced its schizophrenia through neoliberalism. The schizo has become the paraphilic obsession of Nietzsche's last man. Its flood of more and more objects has subjects able to muster less and less desire, as seen in the Japanese Lost Decade of stagflation, when a torrent of perversions coincided with a suicide epidemic. The dominant feelings today are probably anxiety or depression (Plan C, "We Are All Very Anxious").

They are expressed as vulnerability in the pervasiveness of trauma, as a constant low-level distress, and through a generalization of contingency. Demonstrating the significance of this shift: "go play outside" is a breath of fresh air to the bored but fails to make the depressive budge. Neoliberalism turns the depressive into the paranoiac through a program of exposure, which unfolds the subject to reveal new surfaces to penetrate. Despite this, the negative project of the process of schizophrenia ("collapsing a filthy drainage pipe") is as necessary as ever (AO, 341). But just as Lenin declared the revolutionary affirmation "All the power to the Soviets!" counterrevolutionary after a certain time, it is time to retire the slogan "Liberate the flows!"

Militant discussions of infrastructure, blockage, and interruption are refreshing—since the first "free" laborers threw a shoe in the machine, sabotage has been an important tactic of resistance. But with the elliptical dynamics of capitalism, which poses its own limits only to overcome them for a profit, interruptions cannot be an end unto themselves (230–31). Every economic system is "a system of interruptions" that works by breaking down (36–37, 151, 192). One needs to look behind the old social democratic criticism of productivism, "even pollution, cigarettes, prisons, logging, napalm, and nuclear warheads are counted in the Gross Domestic Production," to see why (Kennedy, *Remarks at the University of Kansas*). Antiproduction, which prevents specific realizations of value in a systematic way, is "at the heart of production itself, and conditioning this production" (235). Potlatch and ritualized warfare are indigenous means of antiproduction that prevent the hoarding that could lead to despotism (Maus, *The Gift*; Clastres, *Society against the State*). Aristocratic glorious expenditure made sure that everything was owed to the king (Bataille, "Notion of Expenditure").

Marx reminds us that capitalists dip into their own capital stock at the expense of expanded reproduction, but wasting money on the "political–military–industrial complex" guarantees the smooth advance of the system as a whole (235).

What interruption is revolutionary? The mold was set by Marx, who proposed "expropriating the expropriators" (*Capital*, chapter 32). "Direct action at the point of production" would intervene in the apparatus of capture where the earth, activity, and objects are first coded by the state as territory, work, and money or decoded by capitalism as flows of land, labor, and capital (TP, 437–60). But if "societies are determined by their mode of anti-production (and not a mode of production)," then action should be taken at the points of capitalist antiproduction (D, 135). Extending this line of argumentation, the avant-garde taunts the world with a claim: "capitalism defeated traditional societies because it was more exciting than they were, but now there is something more exciting than capitalism, itself: its destruction" (Bernadette Corporation, *Get Rid of Yourself*). Though this position is condemned by Leninists as infantile leftism, it is the realization of Deleuze and Guattari's critique of therapy culture—clinicians say that one matures out of the depressive position by learning an ambivalent balance of love and hate, which helps delay gratification (Joseph, "Projective Identification," 99). But is that not the alienation of the worker from the fruits of his labor, Deleuze and Guattari protest, the fundamental separation of a desiring subject from her means of satisfaction (AO, 70–75)? Think of an old German rock song, "Macht Kaputt, Was Euch Kaputt Macht" by Ton Steine Scherben, an anarchocommunist band connected to the squatter scene and the Red Army Faction (before it went underground). As cheap as it sounds, perhaps the cure for depressive disinterest is the thrill of "destroying what destroys you."

Substance: Political Anthropology,
Not Technoscience

"Science does not think," Heidegger sensationally claims in his 1952 lecture *What Is Called Thinking?* A year later, Gaston Bachelard makes an opposing scandalous assertion in *Le Matérialisme Rationnel* that "science does not get the philosophy it deserves" (20). What science needs, Bachelard says, is a science that produces objects for thought. One such approach is the "nomad science" of *A Thousand Plateaus,* which forms a direct response to Heidegger's challenge that "we are still not thinking" (*Thinking?,* 6). Nomad science poses problems in clarifying what is really going on in states of affairs (WP, 155–62). In posing better problems, instead of trying to solve them, science invites a range of potential solutions (80–83). "Like a compass, not a blueprint," the saying goes, which is only useful for those who take the time to learn the terrain. In following some technological lines, humans tend to co-evolve with their technological counterparts, or make an even stronger claim: certain technologies produce new peoples (TP, 404–15). So beyond problems, the science of nomads is more an anthropology (or even a geography). Here it may be helpful to consider Deleuze's point about Pascal's Wager in *Nietzsche and Philosophy,* which he says is not a theological question but an anthropological query about how it would be to live without god. The story about nomad scientists and their cousins, the metallurgical smiths, is mostly a history of their appreciation for the singularities of matter, just as Heidegger says the thinking cabinetmaker does when turning each knot and warp to its advantage.

Deleuze and Guattari's autopsy of Oedipus demonstrated the need for anthropology. Their method was analytically clear: dissect him with an internal critique of psychoanalysis and then an external of anthropology. From the first, all they could determine was Oedipus's illegitimate birth, which was already a public secret. It was only through the subsequent historical materialist explanation for Oedipus's emergence that they could plot his demise. We deserve a new anthropology, especially if we plan to commit an act of sedition against the whole world. It will not be born out of a new Enlightenment. Anthropology's Enlightenment father Kant paired anthropology with geography to generate the first scientific classification of race (and white racial superiority) (Bernasconi, "Who Invented the Concept of Race?"). Borrowing from his philosophical work, he lectured on the topic for forty years (1756–97) and published a foundational text, *Anthropology from a Pragmatic Point of View* (Eze, "Color of Reason"). Even anti-Semitic Heidegger knew that reorganizing philosophy along the lines of a succession of psychologies in human history was a grave error—though his negative anthropology leaves the door open to the wild phenomenological speculation of Agamben, Stiegler, and Virno (Balibar, "Subjection and Subjectivation," 2–9). Rather, we need to return to structuralism, if for no other reason than *American anthropology was never (post)structuralist*. Such a provocation is not an attempt to be retro; it is a rejection of the postmodern "reflexive turn" as thirty years lost to naval gazing (Viveiros de Castro, *Cannibal Metaphysics*, 98–100).

Why not a structuralist political anthropology? Viveiros de Castro says that the opening move would be to shatter anthropology as the "mirror of society," which is to say, to shift the crosshairs from psychoanalysis to anthropology to write an *Anti-Narcissus* (*Cannibal Metaphysics*, 40–45). There are a few Deleuzian anthropologists who still take seriously the structuralist project of studying the other: Philippe Descola, Eduardo Kohn, Patrice Maniglier, and Eduardo Viveiros de Castro, to name a few. Only with their help can we overturn the mode of production, perhaps learning from the cannibalist Araweté and Tupinambá's "metaphysics of predation" (*Cannibal Metaphysics,* 142–44). Yet even these anthropologists need to get beyond the naturalist's impulse simply to catalog everything that they see. For even they are struck with their discipline's postcolonial guilt and are content to paint their subjects' lines of becoming in a connectivist "generalized chromaticism" only a few shades from productivism (45, 161). Like Deleuze and Guattari's remarks on Freud as the Martin Luther and Adam Smith of psychology, these anthropologists remain imprisoned by their own states of affairs—until they produce a body to perform an autopsy, *Anti-Narcissus* pulls its punches. And without a critique, it remains too close to "a bizarre mixture of ontology and anthropology, metaphysics and humanism, theology and atheism" (NP, 183). Our conspiracy demands more than knowing how the other conditions herself through the enemy, even if it is how they eat each other; it is a communism that wants to consume the flesh and blood of the entire cosmos.

Nomadism: Barbarian, Not Pastoral

At first blush, nomadism appears pastoral. Deleuze's works constitute one great "horse opera," as the animals appear in more than half of his published work. One question motivates his obsession: what can a horse do? This is an affective inquiry into their capacities and not their meaning:

> take the horse, the apocalyptic beast, as an example: the horse that laughs, in Lawrence; the horse that sticks his head through the window and looks at you, in Kafka; the horse "that is the sun," in Artaud; or even the ass that says *YeaYuh*, in Nietzsche—these are all figures that constitute so many symbols through the building-up of forces, through the constitution of compounds of power. (ECC, 134)

Deleuze chastises Freud for making Little Hans's fear of horses into an image of the father, when it is really a desire to escape to the street (ECC, 64). Horses appear as the first weapons, whose speed is essential to establishing the asymmetrical relation between nomads and the state (TP, 396). When combined with inventions, such as the stirrup or the photograph, horses generate the peculiar movement of speed through immobilization—the voyages in situ of the knight who sleeps on his horse and Muybridge's *Sallie Gardner at a Gallop* (D, 74–75; C1, 5–6). They can be the cause of madness, such the public beating of horses that scarred Dostroyevsky's memory and triggered Nietzsche's break with reality (TP, 257). Yet there is little of ontological import about the horse itself; it takes "the earth" to slow one down through an "artificial reterritorialization" to give any given horse "a particular substance to the content, a particular code to the utterances, a particular limit to becoming, a particular indicative mood (present, past, future) to time" (ECC, 72). As such, the warhorse is far more like a wolf than a workhorse, which is the younger sibling of the ox (TP, 256–57).

The nomads that will dissolve capitalism are not cowboys but barbarians. Not self-attributed but a smear, the term *barbarian* was invented by Hellenistic Greeks as onomatopoeia for the blabber of those who could not speak their language (Padgen, *Fall of Natural Man*, 16). Lacking the capacity for reason, barbarian is used to paint certain foreigners as utterly black and without a single virtue. Not all strangers are vilified by the citizens of empire. Rather, barbarians have two defining characteristics: they refuse to be educated in the language of the *polis* and they act with a savage roughness that exceeds the boundaries of appropriateness (Crisso and Odoteo, *Barbarians*, 40–42). The first jams the usual logocentric means of recognition that would extend them the communal rights of being a human (Padgen, *Fall of Natural Man*, 16); the second banishes them to the uncivilized realm of beasts that lacks decorum, protocol, and restraint (17–18). Nomads are perfectly satisfied with such a one-sided story. What initially appears as an insulting depiction of their limited capacities instead is a definition of how they avoid capture. Barbarians can continue their siege as long as the likes of Hegel, "an honest subject of the Prussian state," cannot apprehend "a completely autonomous, sovereign, uncompromising opposition—a multiplicity that does not allow itself to be enrolled in any synthesis" (Crisso and Odoteo, *Barbarians*, 14). The outside to the new "socially conscious" economy, barbarians avoid the liberal trap of tolerance, compassion, and respect. The only risk is that their ferocity will abate and their passion subside.

The Call of the Outside

Distribution: The Outside, Not Nomos

Cows offer the clearest picture of crowned anarchy, also called "nomadic distribution" (DR, 41; TP, 158). When set out to pasture, they practice *auto-nomy* by following a self-regulated *nomos*, the customary distribution in open space ("in general an unlimited space; it can be a forest, meadows beside rivers, a mountain slope," says philologist Emmanuel Laroche on page 116 of his etymological study) that "crowns" whatever is unique to each landscape, as in livestock feeding on a particular patch of grass and leaving excrement to fertilize the soil anew. *Nomos* is part of a larger constellation of *nem-* words examined by Laroche, including nomads and distribution *(nomos)*, customary law *(nomos)*, melody *(nomos)*, pasture or sphere of command *(nomos)*, roaming *(nomas*, the basis for nomad), pasture *(nemo)*, inhabitant *(naetees)*, territory *(nemeesis)*, governor *(nomarchees)*, and law *(nomoi)*. Most controversial about Laroche's argument is his claim that Greek is the only of the Indo-European languages to be pastoral, which casts the Solonic sense of *nomos* as statist distribution as a betrayal of its nomadic roots. Over the generations, *nomos* loses its nomadic heritage to become the administrative appropriation, distribution, and use of land (22–29, 115–24, 178–205). During this time, *nomos* is combined with the household *(oikos)* to name economics; first mentioned by Phocylides in a poem where he compares women to animals: to dogs, bees, free-range pigs, and long-maned horses (Edmonds, *Elegy and Iambus,* 173–74). (Phocylides suggests that his friend marry the bee because she is a good housekeeper—*oikonomos agathe*; 174.) But Marx shows in chapter 7 of *Capital* that he knows that "what distinguishes the worst architect from the best of bees is this, that the architect raises his structure in imagination before he erects it in reality." Certainly there is a residual speciesism in Marx's remark, as animals' experience of the world *(Umwelt)* is sophisticated enough to produce many things ("art does not wait for human beings to begin") (TP, 320). Yet there is a considerable difference in how humans and cows crown the space that they occupy. As such, we should be concerned more by how each constructs the world than by the excrement with which they consecrate it.

Marx's son-in-law Paul Lafargue demonstrates in his *Social and Philosophical Studies* how *nomos* was turned against the barbarians. Land first "distributed by lot, with the aid of pebbles," is set under the watch of Nemesis, the goddess of just distribution (125; Laroche, *Histoire,* 89–106). *Nomos* continues to affirm its groundlessness when it is played like a game of chance at the table of the gods, with the dice affirming aleatory points that fracture the sky and fall back to a broken earth (DR, 284). Lafargue posits that the great betrayal appears when justice, born out of equality, sanctions the inequalities of land distributed by right and not luck *(Social and Philosophical Studies,* 133–34, 129–30). No longer the protector of nomads, Nemesis inflicts the death penalty "against those who menace property" for the purpose of "teaching the barbarians to trample under foot their noble sentiments of equality and brotherhood"

(130–31). Lafargue thus demands a communist revolution that suppresses private property to banish "the most frightful nightmare which ever tortured sad civilized humanity," the idea of nomic justice (134).

There are two outsides to the state: one a worldwide union, the other a fragmented resistance (TP, 381). To Deleuze and Guattari, this exteriority demonstrates the irreducibility of the *nomos* to the law. If there is anything to this notion, it is not found in a form of exteriority but in the fact of the outside—that there will always be nondenumerable groups (469–73), that there are flows that even the best axiomatic can never master (468–69), and that power now produces more than it can repress (F, 28–29). This is the true meaning of "deterritorialization" and "the infinite speed of thought"—each concept confirms the extraordinary powers of the outside (AO, 105; WP, 21, 35–38, 42). The difficulty is that "one cannot write sufficiently in the name of an outside" because it "has no image, no signification, no subjectivity" (TP, 23). How then to link with the outside? The simplest way is to fashion a war machine as a relation to the outside (TP, 376–77). Another path to "a new relation to the outside" may be found in a fissured planet that spews fires that consume the world (DI, 156, 158–59). Such deterritorializations unleash movements that "cease to be terrestrial" when "the religious Nome blooms and dissolves" and "the singing of the birds is replaced by combinations of water, wind, clouds, and fog" (TP, 327).

The outside appears like Frankenstein's monster, with a crack of lightning late into the dreary night while the atomist's rain patters away from the outside. Its darkness does not come from void worship or an existentialist reckoning with nothingness. Flashing brilliantly as a shock to thought, it appears as the "bearer of a problem" that paints the world black with dread (DR, 140). This movement grounds thought as "the relationship with the outside" (DI, 255). Exteriority here is not some transcendent light or yawning void. Rather, the outside opens out to a new milieu, like cracking the window in a house. The outside is seldom as pleasant as a breeze, however, as it invades in all its alien force. Thought here has a choice, to represent or intensify; the latter follows Paul Klee's famous formula: "not to render the visible, but to render visible" (FB, 144). It amplifies the impinging power of the outside to cause a horrible discord that splits apart the harmonies of reason sung in the halls of state thought (DI, 259–60). Such philosophy does not sing, it screams in the analogical language of "expressive movements, paralinguistic signs, breaths" (FB, 93). The outside howls with an "open mouth as a shadowy abyss" (51).

Politics: Cataclysmic, Not Molecular

"The revolutionary was molecular, and so was the counter-revolution," Tiqqun prophetically declares (*Introduction to Civil War*, 200). Yet the "molecular revolution" actually begins with Proust, who writes in *Sodom and Gomorrah* of three levels of sexuality: straights, gays, and queers. The first two types connect "molar" lines between fixed objects, each category simply being an inversion of the other (AO, 68–71). The third draws a "transversal" molecular line between the unspecified, partial, and flux of flows "unaware of persons, aggregates, and laws, and of images, structures, and symbols" (70–71, 311). For a long time, the love that dare not speak its name hid with other queer things made up of "very different mechanisms, thresholds, sites, and observers" (WP, 78). But counterculture exposed the secret, which is to say, disclosed a molecular line of previously clandestine passions while blossoming into the flower power of the Summer of Love publicly consecrated at Woodstock's Three Days of Peace, Music, and Love. This new world bore what Paolo Virno calls in *Grammar of the Multitude* the liberatory "anti-socialist demands" of "radical criticism of labor," "an accentuated taste for differences" and "the aptitude (at times violent, certainly) for defending oneself from the State, for dissolving the bondage to the State as such" (111). But the life of this molecular line was short. It was put back to work by disco, flexible production, and the Reagan revolution in an odd "communism of capital" (111).

The cataclysm is not an end but a new beginning, the cataclysm of a temporary hell, "itself the effect of an elementary injustice" that sweeps in and out, rather than being an abysmal lake of sulfur where souls burn forever (ECC, 46). It is the apocalypse before its decadent transformation into the system of Judgment (39). Only a revival of this cataclysmic event can end the apocalypse of an "already industrialized organization" that appeared "a Metropolis" by way of "the great military, police, and civil security of a new State" with a "programmed self-glorification" complemented by a "demented installation of an ultimate judiciary and moral power" (44, 46). We know from Nietzsche's *Gay Science* that the impending cataclysm of "breakdown, destruction, ruin" may appear gloomy (279). And it will certainly cover the earth in a blackness darker than the world has ever seen (279). Yet we should greet it with cheer. For the cataclysm brings with it a new dawn worthy of our highest expectations. Though the daybreak may not be bright, we will have escaped the judgment of God, Man, and the World. "At long last our ships may venture out again, venture out to face any danger," because "the sea, *our* sea, lie open again" . . . "perhaps there has never yet been such an 'open sea'" (280).

Cinema: The Powers of the False, Not the Forces of Bodies

Bodies are a well-composed image of power. The body of God (the Sacrament of Jesus). The body of a saint (the pierced corpse of the martyr). The body of the sovereign (the King's two bodies). The body of the tyrant (Big Brother's face). The social body (the body politic). A body of evidence (the state's case). The idea of society or the world functioning as an organism is well sedimented. In its stupidest form, it posits a resemblance between the human body and society. Just as various organisms interact to form an organism as a functional whole, it states, society is the cooperation of various social organs. The body provides an image for the much-talked-about "body without organs," the great inspiration for Deleuze, who says that if we are to believe in the world, "give me a body then" (C2, 189).

The body is not really the enemy, the organism is. Some would have bodies appear through their opposites, locked in eternal combat—as the sinner and their Eternal Savior, the regicide and the King, the criminal and the Law (TP, 108). But as an organism, the body is put to use for extracting "useful labor," either as a product of work (where organs are connected to the technical machines of the capitalism) or self-reproduction (where organs are connected to the social machines of the species) (AO, 54). The image of the body as an organism might appear as a step forward, as it invokes a form of ecological thinking of interconnected systems. But we are only interested in the body as a frustrating set of resistances, "obstinate and stubborn," as it "forces us to think, and forces us to think what is concealed from thought, life" (C2, 189). This is why it is said that "we do not even know what a body can do." But with the relative ease in which the body has been confused for an organism, perhaps it is time to abandon the image of the body completely. Stop thinking like lawyers, who try cases only after a body has been found. There is a simple reason: the point is not to construct a body without organs (organization, organism, . . .) but organs without a body. We only get outside the productivist logic of accumulation when "at last the disappearance of the visible body is achieved" (C2, 190).

Against the state's body of evidence: "The 'true world' does not exist," and even if it did, "it would be inaccessible, impossible to describe, and, if it could be described, would be useless, superfluous" (C2, 137). The conspiracy against this world begins with time, which "puts truth in crisis" (130). This is the fundamental problem of the "body of the law" described by Derrida whereby the law must continually rule against what it previously established as the truth (and thus its own authority) ("Force of Law"). It is these moments that reveal an in-effectivity of the truth—denouncing states, nations, or races as fictions does little to dislodge their power, however untrue the historical or scientific justifications for them might be (Seshadri, *Desiring Whiteness*). The state is nothing but these *"not-necessarily true pasts,"* the founding mythologies that fictionalize the origin of states and nations of people (C2, 131). This is the power generated only between the true and the false: what Deleuze calls "the real." The importance of the real is central, as trying to use truth to dispute the false does not work: those who denounce the illegal violence used to found legal orders are quickly dismissed or jailed, and the many climate scientists who harangue the public about the truth of global warming fail to spur policy change.

Cinema "takes up the problem of truth and attempts to resolve it through purely cinematic means" (Lambert, *Nonphilosophy,* 93). There are films that go beyond metaphor and analogy, operating instead through a realism of the false. This is not the epic cinema of Brecht or Lang, whose dissimulation and relativism ultimately return the morality of judgment through the viewer. It is a realism of what escapes the body, presenting something it cannot perceive on its own—not different worlds but realities that exist in the present (though not currently lived) that confirm reality by weakening it. Deleuze finds that the elusive truth of postwar cinema does not prevent the existence of a "truthful man" but the "forger" as the character of new cinema (C2, 132). The forger refuses the moral origins of truth and frustrates the return to judgment (C2, 138–39). The realism of the false shows us love through the eyes of a serial killer (Grandrieux's *Sombre*), gives us the real thrill of self-destruction (Gavras's *Our Day Will Come*), unleashes the cruelty of nature against the cool logic of liberal patriarchy (von Trier's *Anti-Christ*), and solicits us in the horrifying conspiracies of a new flesh (Cronenberg's *Videodrome*).

The Sensible: Indiscernibility, Not Experience

The senses think when the boundary between the imaginary and the real collapses. This is what happens whenever the suspension of disbelief continues outside the frame (C2, 169). But the suspension carries on only as long as it is not whittled down to a narrow proposition through "infinite specification" (DR, 306). It expands by establishing a "distinct yet indiscernible" proximity (TP, 279–80, 286). In this strange zone of indiscernibility, figuration recedes—it is right before our eyes, but we lose our ability to clarify the difference between a human body, a beast, and meat (FB, 22–27). There is no mystical outside, just the unrelenting intrusion of "the fact that we are not yet thinking" (C2, 167). This is because experience is itself not thought but merely the provocation to think—a reminder of the insufferable, the impossibility of continuing the same, and the necessity of change.

"Knowledge is not made for understanding; it is made for cutting," says Foucault ("Nietzsche, Genealogy, History," 88). Neither is sense. The best sense is a sensation, a provocation, that introduces insufficiency (L, 50–58). So instead of adequate conceptions, we spread insufficient sensations. This insufficiency does not carry the weight of inevitability. It may begin with a petulant indecisiveness, such as Bartleby's "I would prefer not to," but it must not end there. The greatest danger is that indecision consumes us and we become satisfied for one reason or another, withering like Bartleby in jail cells of our own making. Our communism demands that we actively conspire under the cover of the secret; for there is nothing more active than the Death of the World. Our hatred propels us. Just as "an adventure that erupts in sedentary groups" through "the call of the outside," our sense that the world is intolerable is what compels us to build our own barbarian siege engines to attack the new Metropolis that stands in Judgment like a Heaven on Earth (DI, 259).

Conclusion

AS A PROLEGOMENA to any future negativity in Deleuze, this book risks being too condensed. The moves I make are quick, and many will appear perverse to friends of the Joyous Deleuze. For justification: the force of thought is a matter of style and not the specification of concepts, or to use proper names, Nietzsche contra Kant (DR, 5, 13, 306). I therefore build my case through formulations that are "rigorous yet anexact" like Deleuze's, whose "essentially not accidentally inexact" concepts modulate enough between books to deserve different names (TP, 367, 555). I promote minor terms through extensive footnotes generated through a deep reading of Deleuze across the breadth of his complete works. So on one hand, I am so indebted to Deleuze that one could say that I merely provide a new nomenclature for old Deleuzian concepts. On the other, this is a book that Deleuze himself could never have written, as his age was not one of obligatory positivity, distributed management, and stifling transparency. My basic argument is that a new untimeliness in a time not Deleuze's own requires a negative project that his work introduces but does not sustain: the Death of this World.

The end of this world is the third in a succession of deaths—the Death of God, the Death of Man, and now the Death of this

World. This is not a call to physically destroy the world. The Death of God did not call for the assault of priests or the burning of churches, and the Death of Man did not propose genocide or the extinction of our species. Each death denounces a concept as insufficient, critiques those who still believe in it, and demands its removal as an object of thought. In the Death of Man, we learned that the human sciences were impotent in the face of the systemic injustices of this world. Rather, Foucault shows how expert inquiry makes exploitation, sexism, racism, poverty, violence, and war into the constitutive elements of how humanity defends itself. He shows that attempts to save this humanity created a biopower that "makes live and lets die," which paradoxically administers life through "a power to expose a whole population to death" that tends toward wars of all-out destruction (Foucault, *History of Sexuality,* 135–37). Elaborating on this condition, subsequent theorists say that we have already been killed but have not yet died, making us an "already dead" that makes us already ready to adopt a revolutionary orientation that sacrifices our current time and space for a new, not-yet-realized future (Cazdyn, *Already Dead,* 9). Seen from this perspective, runaway climate change, the Sixth Extinction, and many other impending catastrophes are all essential parts of this world. The Death of this World admits the insufficiency of previous attempts to save it and instead poses a revolutionary gamble: only by destroying this world will we release ourselves of its problems. This does not mean moving to the moon, but that we give up on all the reasons given for saving the world. In my own announcement of the death of this world, I propose critiques of connectivity and positivity, a theory of contraries, the exercise of intolerance, and the conspiracy of communism.

Contemporary Deleuze scholarship tends to be connectivist and productivist. Connectivism is the world-building integration into an expanding web of things. As an organizational logic, it is the promiscuous inclusion of seemingly unrelated elements into a single body to expand its capacities. Academics are not alone in endorsing connectivism—I argue that connectivism drives Google's geopolitical strategy of global influence, which proceeds through a techno-affirmationist desire to annex everything. Commentators use different names for their webs of connections, such as rhizomes, assemblages, networks, material systems, or *dispositifs*. I simply call them "this world" and plot for its destruction. Productivism links up with the autonomous, ceaseless autoproduction of the real. The most naive productivists sentimentally cherish creation and novelty for their own sake, whether as dewy-eyed admiration for the complexity of nature or a staunch Voltairine defense of all types of diversity. The productivists worthy of criticism are those who, in the name of "finding something about this world to believe in," affirm what is given as if this wretched world already included all materials for a better one. I find that in relinquishing the power of destruction, they can only capitalize on production through the logics of accumulation and reproduction. So in founding a new world on the terms of the old, its horizon expands barely beyond what already exists. The alternative I propose is finding reasons to destroy this world.

The greatest crime of joyousness is tolerance. While mentioning tolerance may have marked one as a radical in Deleuze's time, Wendy Brown argues in *Regulating Aversion* that liberal tolerance is now essential to the grammar of empire's "domestic discourse of ethnic, racial, and sexual regulation, on the one hand, and as an international discourse of Western supremacy and imperialism on the other" (1, 7). Today's tolerant are to blame for a "liberal Deleuze," such as William Connolly, who names Deleuze as an antirevolutionary who inspires his belief that "transformation is neither needed nor in the cards today; what is needed is creative modes of *intervention* posed at several strategic sites in the service of reducing economic inequality, foster intra- and inter-state pluralism, and promoting ecological sanity" in his book on pluralism (*Pluralism,* 159). Deleuze criticized a similar position many decades ago when denouncing the media-hungry form of the *Nouveaux Philosophes,* who had "inscribed themselves perfectly well on the electoral grid . . . from which everything fades away" ("On the New Philosophers," 40–41). Liberal Deleuzians can be criticized accordingly—for endorsing the usual abstractions of the Law and the State that hide the workings of power; for denouncing Marxism "not so much because real struggles would have made new enemies, new problems and new means arise, but because THE revolution must be declared impossible"; and for reviving the subject as part of a general martyrology. What stands between liberalism and revolution is intolerance, but in a peculiar way. Intolerance arises out of this world as "something intolerable in the world" to prove that there is "something unthinkable in thought" (C2, 169). Which is to say, it is when we find it all unbearable that we realize "it can no longer think a world or think itself" (170). This is where the Dark Deleuze parts ways with the joyful by inviting the death of this world. There are many fellow travelers of revolutionary intolerance, including Wendy Brown and Herbert Marcuse. Newton argues in his autobiography *Revolutionary Suicide* that the revolutionary task is to risk one's life for the chance of "changing intolerable conditions" (5). In his essay on "repressive tolerance," Marcuse extends tolerance only to the left, subversion, and revolutionary violence and proposes a militant intolerance of the right, this world, and "benevolent neutrality." Together, they express the dark truth of the intolerable as the lived present of being trapped by something so unbearable, so impossible, that it must be destroyed. To be completely clear: the point is not to grow obstinate but to find new ways to end our suffocating perpetual present.

Darkness advances the secret as an alternative to the liberal obsession with transparency. Foucault smartly identifies transparency's role in the "science of the police," which is used in the task of maintaining order through the collusion between the state and capital from liberalism's beginnings in the German notion of the police state through to contemporary biopolitics (*Security, Territory, Population*). The conspiracy is against the consistency of everything being in its proper place, and the secret is the fact that nothing is as it seems. Such a conspiracy is not the pursuit of the ineffable or sublime, as it is neither esoteric nor mystical. It circulates as an open secret that retains its secrecy only by operating against connectivism through the principle of selective engagement. The lesson to be taken is that "we all must live double lives": one full of the compromises we make with the present, and the other in which we plot to undo them. The struggle is to keep one's cover identity from taking over. There are those whose daily drudgery makes it difficult to contribute to the conspiracy, though people in this position are far more likely to have secret dealings on the side. Others are given ample opportunities but still fail to grow the secret, the most extreme example being those who live their lives "with nothing to hide," often declaring that they are "an open book." Some treat the conspiracy as a form of hobbyism, working to end the world only after everything else has been taken care of— the worst being liberal communists, who exploit so much in the morning that they can give half of it back as charity in the afternoon. And then there are those who escape. Crafting new weapons while withdrawing from the demands of the social, they know that cataclysm knows nothing of the productivist logic of accumulation or reproduction. Escape need not be dreary, even if they are negative. Escape is never more exciting than when it spills out into the streets, where trust in appearances, trust in words, trust in each other, and trust in this world all disintegrate in a mobile zone of indiscernibility (Fontaine, "Black Bloc"). It is in these moments of opacity, insufficiency, and breakdown that darkness most threatens the ties that bind us to this world.

Acknowledgments

Thanks to Mark Purcell, Keith Harris, Cheryl Gilge, and everyone at the University of Washington for the opportunity to write this book. I am grateful for critical feedback from Alex Galloway, Geert Lovink, Jose Rosales, Matt Applegate, Alejandro de Acosta, and an anonymous reviewer. Finally, I am indebted to the numerous people who stood beside me at the intellectual and political barricades throughout the project, perhaps too numerous to name, except for one: Eva Della Lana.

Bibliography

Althusser, Louis. *Philosophy of the Encounter: Later Writings, 1978–1987.* 1993/1994. Translated by G. M. Goshgarian. Edited by Oliver Corpet and François Matheron. New York: Verso, 2006.

Anonymous. "De l'Hypothèse Cybernétique." *Tiqqun* 2 (2001): 223–339.

Anonymous. "May 1968 Graffiti." In *Bureau of Public Secrets,* translated by Ken Knabb. 2006. http://www.bopsecrets.org/CF/graffiti.htm.

Bachelard, Gaston. *Le Matérialisme Rationnel.* Paris: Presses Universitaires de France, 1953.

Badiou, Alain. "Althusser: Subjectivity without a Subject." 1998. In *Metapolitics,* translated by Jason Barker, 58–67. New York: Verso, 2005.

Balibar, Étienne. "Subjection and Subjectivation." In *Supposing the Subject,* edited by Joan Copjec, 1–15. New York: Verso, 1994.

———. *The Philosophy of Marx.* 1993. Translated by Chris Turner. New York: Verso, 1995.

Bataille, Georges. "The Notion of Expenditure." 1933. In *Visions of Excess: Selected Writings, 1927–1939,* translated by Allan Stoekl, Carl R. Lovin, and Donald M. Leslie Jr., 167–81. Minneapolis: University of Minnesota Press, 1985.

Bernadette Corporation, dir. *Get Rid of Yourself.* New York: Electronic Arts Intermix, 2003.

Bernasconi, Robert. "Who Invented the Concept of Race? Kant's Role in the Enlightenment Construction of Race." In *Race,* edited by Robert Bernasconi, 11–36. Malden, Mass.: Blackwell, 2001.

Bey, Hakim. *The Temporary Autonomous Zone, Ontological Anarchy, Poetic Terrorism.* 2nd ed. Brooklyn, N.Y.: Autonomedia, 2003.

Brown, Wendy. *Regulating Aversion: Tolerance in the Age of Identity and Empire*. Princeton, N.J.: Princeton University Press.

Buiness Insider. "Google Chairman: 'The Internet Will Disappear.'" 2015. http://www.businessinsider.com/google-chief-eric-schmidt-the -internet-will-disappear-2015-1.

Butler, Samuel. *Erewhon: or, Over the Range*. 1872. London: AC Fifield, 1910. http://www.gutenberg.org/files/1906/1906-h/1906-h.htm.

Cazdyn, Eric. *The Already Dead: The New Time of Politics, Culture, and Illness*. Durham, N.C.: Duke University Press, 2012.

Chaplin, Charlie, dir. *Modern Times*. New York: Criterion Collection, 1936.

Clastres, Pierre. *Society against the State*. 1974. Translated by Robert Hurley and Abe Stein. New York: Zone Books, 1987.

Cohen, Jared, and Eric Schmidt. *The New Digital Age: Reshaping the Future of People, Nations, and Business*. New York: Doubleday, 2013.

Connolly, William E. *Pluralism*. Durham, N.C.: Duke University Press, 2005.

Crisso and Odoteo. *Barbarians: The Disordered Insurgence*. Anonymous translation. 2003. http://theanarchistlibrary.org/library/crisso-and -odoteo-barbarians-the-disordered-insurgence.pdf.

Debord, Guy. "The Bad Old Days Will End." 1963. In *Leaving the 20th Century: The Incomplete Work of the Situationist International*, translated by Christopher Gray, 33–37. London: Rebel Press, 1998.

DeLanda, Manuel. *Intensive Science and Virtual Philosophy*. London: Continuum, 2002.

Deleuze, Gilles. *Cinema 1: The Movement-Image*. 1983. Translated by Hugh Tomlinson and Barbara Habberjam. Minneapolis: University of Minnesota Press, 1986.

——. *Cinema 2: The Time-Image*. 1985. Translated by Hugh Tomlinson and Robert Galeta. Minneapolis: University of Minnesota Press, 1989.

——. *Desert Islands and Other Texts, 1953–1974*. 2002. New York: Semiotext(e), 2004.

——. *Difference and Repetition*. 1968. Translated by Paul Patton. New York: Columbia University Press, 1994.

——. *Empiricism and Subjectivity: An Essay on Hume's Theory of Human Nature*. 1953. Translated by Constantin V. Boundas. New York: Columbia University Press, 1995.

——. *Essays Critical and Clinical*. 1993. Translated by Daniel W. Smith and Michael A. Greco. Minneapolis: University of Minnesota Press, 1997.

——. *Expressionism in Philosophy: Spinoza*. 1968. Translated by Martin Joughin. New York: Zone Books, 1990.

——. *The Fold: Leibniz and the Baroque*. 1988. Translated by Tom Conley. Minneapolis: University of Minnesota Press, 1993.

——. *Foucault*. 1986. Translated by Seán Hand. Minneapolis: University of Minnesota Press, 1988.

——. *Francis Bacon: The Logic of Sensation*. 1981. Translated by Daniel W. Smith. Minneapolis: University of Minnesota Press, 2005.

——. *Logic of Sense*. 1969. Translated by Mark Lester, with Charles Stivale. Edited by Constantin V. Boundas. New York: Columbia University Press, 1990.

——. *Negotiations: 1972–1990*. 1990. Translated by Martin Joughin. New York: Columbia University Press, 1995.

——. *Nietzsche and Philosophy*. 1962. Translated by Hugh Tomlinson. New York: Columbia University Press, 2006.

——. "On the New Philosophers and a More General Problem." Interview with Bertrand Augst. Translated by Bertrand Augst. *Discourse* 20, no. 3 (1998): 34–43.

——. *Proust and Signs*. 1964. Translated by Richard Howard. London: Continuum, 2000.

——. *Pure Immanence: A Life*. 1995. Translated by Anne Boyman. New York: Zone Books, 2001.

——. *Spinoza: Practical Philosophy*. 1970. Translated by Robert Hurley. San Francisco: City Lights Books, 1988.

——. *Two Regimes of Madness: Texts and Interviews 1975–1995*. 2001. Translated by Amed Hodges and Mike Taormina. Edited by David Lapoujade. Los Angeles, Calif.: Semiotext(e), 2007.

Deleuze, Gilles, and Félix Guattari. *Anti-Oedipus*. 1972. Translated by Robert Hurley, Mark Seem, and Helen R. Lane. Minneapolis: University of Minnesota Press, 1977.

——. *Kafka: Toward a Minor Literature*. 1975. Translated by Dana Polan. Minneapolis: University of Minnesota Press, 1986.

——. *A Thousand Plateaus*. 1980. Translated by Brian Massumi. Minneapolis: University of Minnesota Press, 1987.

——. *What Is Philosophy?* 1991. Translated by Hugh Tomlinson and Graham Burchell. New York: Columbia University Press, 1994.

Deleuze, Gilles, and Claire Parnet. 1977. *Dialogues 2*, rev. ed., translated by Hugh Tomlinson and Barbara Habberjam. New York: Columbia University Press, 2007.

Derrida, Jacques. "Force of Law: The Mystical Foundation of Authority." 1989. In *Deconstruction and the Possibility of Justice,* edited by Drucilla Cornell et al., 3–66. New York: Routledge, 1992.

Dumézil, Georges. *Mitra-Varuna: An Essay on Two Indo-European Representations of Sovereignty.* 1984. Translated by Derek Coltman. New York: Zone Books, 1988.

Edelman, Lee. *No Future: Queer Theory and the Death Drive.* Durham, N.C.: Duke University Press, 2004.

Edmonds, John Maxwell. *Elegy and Iambus, Being the Remains of All the Greek Elegiac and Iambic Poets from Callinus to Crates, Excepting the Choliambic Writers, with the Anacreontea.* Vol. 1. Cambridge, Mass.: Harvard University Press, 1931.

Eze, Emmanuel Chudwuki. "The Color of Reason: The Idea of 'Race' in Kant's Anthropology." In *Postcolonial African Philosophy: A Critical Reader,* edited by Emmanuel Chudwuki Eze, 103–31. Cambridge, Mass.: Blackwell, 1997.

Flaxman, Gregory. *Gilles Deleuze and the Fabulation of Philosophy.* Minneapolis: University of Minnesota Press, 2011.

———. "Politics and Ontology: A Review of Nathan Widder: *Political Theory after Deleuze.*" *Postmodern Culture* 24, no. 2 (2014), https://muse.jhu.edu/article/580775.

Flint, Jim. "Michel Serres' Angels: A Modern Myth." *Mute* 1, no. 4 (1996). http://www.metamute.org/editorial/articles/michel-serres-angels-modern-myth.

Fontaine, Claire. "This Is Not the Black Bloc." 2007. http://www.clairefontaine.ws/pdf/black_bloc_eng.pdf.

Foucault, Michel. *History of Sexuality, Volume 1: An Introduction.* Translated by Robert Hurley. New York: Pantheon Books, 1978.

———. "Nietzsche, Genealogy, History." 1971. In *Language, Counter-Memory, Practice: Selected Essays and Interviews,* translated by Donald F. Bouchard and Sherry Simon, 113–38. Ithaca, N.Y.: Cornell University Press, 1977.

———. *Security, Territory, Population: Lectures at the Collège de France 1977–1978.* 2004. Translated by Graham Burchell. Edited by Michel Senellart. New York: Palgrave Macmillan, 2007.

———. *"Society Must Be Defended": Lectures at the Collège de France, 1975–1976.* 1997. Translated by David Macey. New York: Picador, 2003.

———. "Theatrum Philosophicum." *Critique* 282 (1970): 885–908.

Galloway, Alexander R. *Protocol: How Control Exists after Decentralization.* Cambridge, Mass.: MIT Press, 2004.

Galloway, Alexander R., and Eugene Thacker. *The Exploit: A Theory of Networks.* Minneapolis: University of Minnesota Press, 2007.

Gingrich, Owen, and Albert van Helden, "From *Occhiale* to Printed Page: The Making of Galileo's *Sidereus Nuncius*." *Journal for the History of Astronomy* 34, no. 116 (2003): 251–67.

Grosz, Elizabeth. *Becoming Undone: Darwinian Reflections on Life, Politics, and Art.* Durham, N.C.: Duke University Press, 2011.

Guevara, Ernesto "Che." *Guerilla Warfare.* 1960. Translated by J. P. Morray. Oxford: SR Books, 1997.

Halperin, David, and Valerie Traub. "Beyond Gay Pride." In *Gay Shame,* 3–40. Chicago: University of Chicago Press, 2009.

Hardt, Michael. "The Common in Communism." 2010. http://seminaire.samizdat.net/IMG/pdf/Microsoft_Word_-_Michael_Hardt.pdf.

Hardt, Michael, and Antonio Negri. *Empire.* Cambridge, Mass.: Harvard University Press, 2000.

Heidegger, Martin. *What Is Called Thinking?* 1952. Translated by J. Glenn Gray. New York: Perennial, 1976.

Hevelii, Johannis. *Selenographia sive Lunae Descriptio.* Gdansk, 1647.

Holloway, John. "The Scream." In *Change the World without Taking Power: The Meaning of Revolution Today,* 1–10. London: Pluto Press, 2002.

Invisible Committee. *To Our Friends.* 2014. Translated by Robert Hurley. Los Angeles, Calif.: Semiotext(e), 2015.

Joseph, Betty. "Projective Identification: Some Clinical Aspects." In *Projective Identification: The Fate of a Concept,* edited by Elizabeth Spillius and Edna O'Shaughnessy, 98–111. New York: Routledge, 2012.

Kafka, Franz. *The Trial.* 1925. Translated by Willa and Edwin Muir. New York: Schocken, 1956.

Kant, Immanuel. *Anthropology from a Pragmatic Point of View.* 1798. Translated by Robert B. Louden. Cambridge: Cambridge University Press, 2006.

Kauffman, Stuart. *Reinventing the Sacred: A New View of Science, Reason, and Religion.* New York: Basic Books, 2008.

Kauffman, Stuart, Teppo Felin, Roger Koppl, and Giuseppe Longo. "Economic Opportunity and Evolution: Beyond Landscapes and

Bibliography

Bounded Rationality." *Strategic Entrepreneurship Journal* 8, no. 4 (2014): 269–82.

Kennedy, Robert F. *Remarks at the University of Kansas.* March 18, 1968.

Kissinger, Henry. "The Vietnam Negotiations." *Foreign Affairs* 48, no. 2 (1969): 211–34.

Klossowski, Pierre. "Circulus Vitiosus." Translated by Joseph Kuzma. *The Agonist: A Nietzsche Circle Journal* 2, no. 1 (2009): 31–47.

———. *Nietzsche and the Vicious Circle.* 1969. Translated by Daniel W. Smith. Chicago: University of Chicago Press, 1997.

Kopal, Zdeněk. *The Moon.* Dordrecht, Netherlands: D. Reidel, 1969.

Kubrick, Stanley, dir. *Clockwork Orange.* Burbank, Calif.: Warner Bros. Pictures, 1971.

Lafargue, Paul. *Social and Philosophical Studies.* Translated by Charles H. Kerr. Chicago: Charles H. Kerr, 1910.

Lambert, Gregg. *The Non-philosophy of Gilles Deleuze.* London: Continuum, 2002.

Land, Nick. "Annotated #Accelerate (#2b)." *Urban Future* 2, no. 1 (2014). http://www.ufblog.net/on-accelerate-2b.

———. "Annotated #Accelerate (#3)." *Urban Future* 2, no. 1 (2014). http://www.ufblog.net/annotated-accelerate-3/.

———. "The Dark Enlightenment." In *The Dark Enlightenment.* 2013. http://www.thedarkenlightenment.com/the-dark-enlightenment-by-nick-land/.

———. *Thirst for Annihilation: George Bataille and Virulent Nihilism.* London: Routledge, 1992.

Lang, Fritz, dir. *Metropolis.* 1927. New York: Kino Video, 2004.

Laroche, Emmanuel. *Histoire de la Racine "Nem-" en Grec Ancien.* Paris: Librairie C. Klincksieck, 1949.

Lübke, Wilhelm. *Ecclesiastical Art in Germany during the Middle Ages.* 1852. Translated by I. A. Wheatley. London: Cassell, Petter, and Galpin, 1871.

Luke, Timothy W. *Ecocritique: Contesting the Politics of Nature, Economy, and Culture.* Minneapolis: University of Minnesota Press, 1997.

Lyotard, Jean-François. *Libidinal Economy.* 1974. Translated by Iain Hamilton Grant. London: Athlone, 2004.

Marcuse, Herbert. "Repressive Tolerance." In *A Critique of Pure Tolerance,* 81–117. Boston: Beacon Press, 1965.

Marx, Karl. *Capital: A Critique of Political Economy.* Vol. 1. Translated by Ben Fowkes. Harmondsworth, U.K.: Penguin, 1976.

———. "Ruthless Criticism." Letter to Arnold Ruge, September 1843. In *Marx Engel's Collected Works*, 3. https://www.marxists.org/archive /marx/works/1843/letters/43_09.htm.

Marx, Karl, and Friedrich Engels. *Manifesto of the Community Party*. 1848. Translated by Samuel Moore and Friedrich Engels. 2000. https://www.marxists.org/archive/marx/works/1848/communist -manifesto/ch01.htm.

Maus, Marcel. *The Gift: The Form and Reason for Exchange in Archaic Societies*. 1950. Translated by W. D. Hallis. New York: Routledge, 1990.

Meillassoux, Quentin. *After Finitude: An Essay on the Necessity of Contingency*. 2006. Translated by Ray Brassier. London: Continuum, 2008.

Muybridge, Eadweard, dir. *Sallie Gardner at a Gallop*. 1878.

Newton, Huey. *Revolutionary Suicide*. New York: Writers and Readers, 1973.

Nietzsche, Friedrich. *The Gay Science*. 1887. Translated by Walter Kaufmann. New York: Vintage Books, 1974.

———. *On the Genealogy of Morality*. 1887. Translated by Carol Diethe. Edited by Keith Ansell-Pearson. New York: Cambridge University Press, 1994.

———. *Untimely Meditations*. Translated by R. J. Hollingdale. Edited by Daniel Breazeale. Cambridge: Cambridge University Press, 1997.

Orwell, George. *1984*. New York: Penguin, 1949.

Padgen, Anthony. *The Fall of Natural Man: The American Indian and the Origins of Comparative Ethnology*. Cambridge: Cambridge University Press, 1982.

Plan C. "We Are All Very Anxious." April 4, 2014. http://www.weareplanc .org/blog/we-are-all-very-anxious/.

Proust, Marcel. "Cities of the Plain" [alternative title to "Sodom and Gomorrah"]. 1921. In *Remembrance of Things Past* [alternative title to *In Search of Lost Time*], translated by C. K. Scott Moncrieff, 3–378. New York: Random House, 1932.

Rancière, Jacques. *Dissensus: On Politics and Aesthetics*. Edited and translated by Steven Corcoran. London: Continuum, 2010.

Rice, Condoleezza. *No Higher Honor*. New York: Broadway, 2011.

Rimbaud, Arthur. "A Season in Hell." 1873. Translated by A. S. Kline. http://www.poetryintranslation.com/PITBR/French/Rimbaud3 .htm#anchor_Toc202003798.

Ruddick, Susan. "The Politics of Affect: Spinoza in the Work of Negri and Deleuze." *Theory, Culture, Society* 27, no. 4 (2010): 21–45.

Schumpeter, Joseph Alois. 1942. *Capitalism, Socialism, Democracy.* New York: Harper and Row, 1950.

Serres, Michel. *Angels, a Modern Myth.* Paris: Flammarion, 1995.

Seshadri, Kalpana Rahita (formerly Seshadri-Crooks). *Desiring Whiteness: A Lacanian Analysis of Race.* London: Routledge, 2000.

Spanos, William V. "The Question of Philosophy and *Poiesis* in the Posthistorical Age: Thinking/Imagining the Shadow of Metaphysics." *Boundary 2* 27, no. 1 (2000): 151–74.

Spence-Jones, Henry Donald Maurice. *Early Christianity and Paganism, a.d. 64 to the Peace of the Church in the Fourth Century.* London: Cassell, 1902.

Spinoza, Benedict de. *Ethics.* 1677. Translated by Edwin Curley. New York: Penguin, 2005.

Stengers, Isabelle. *In Catastrophic Times: Resisting the Coming Barbarism.* Translated by Andrew Goffey. London: Open Humanities Press.

Tiqqun. *Introduction to Civil War.* 2001. Translated by Alexander R. Galloway and Jason E. Smith. Los Angeles, Calif.: Semiotext(e), 2010.

Unknown. "Essay upon Crypts." *The Crypt: or, Receptacle for Things Past* 6 (September 1829): 73–77.

Virno, Paolo. *Grammar of the Multitude: For an Analysis of Contemporary Forms of Life.* 2003. Translated by Isabella Bertoletti, James Cascaito, and Andrea Casson. New York: Semiotext(e), 2004.

Viveiros de Castro, Eduardo. *Cannibal Metaphysics: For a Post-structural Anthropology.* 2009. Translated by Peter Skafish. Minneapolis, Minn.: Univocal, 2014.

Williams, Alex, and Nick Srincek. "#Accelerate Manifesto for an Accelerationist Politics." *Critical Legal Thinking.* 2013, http://criticallegalthinking.com/2013/05/14/accelerate-manifesto-for-an-accelerationist-politics/.

Žižek, Slavoj. "The Ongoing 'Soft Revolution.'" *Critical Inquiry* 30, no. 2 (2004): 292–323.

———. *The Sublime Object of Ideology.* New York: Verso, 1989.

Zourabichvili, François. *Gilles Deleuze: A Philosophy of the Event.* 1994. Translated by Kieran Aarons. Edited by Gregg Lambert and Daniel W. Smith. Edinburgh: Edinburgh University Press, 2012.

Andrew Culp is visiting assistant professor of rhetoric studies at Whitman College.